The
Marketing
Imagination

Other books by Theodore Levitt

Innovation in Marketing (1962)

Industrial Purchasing Behavior: A Study of Communication Effects (1964)

Marketing (1964) (with John B. Matthews, Jr., Robert D. Buzzell, and Ronald Frank)

The Marketing Mode (1969)

Marketing: A Contemporary Analysis (1972) (with Robert D. Buzzell, Robert E. M. Nourse, and John B. Matthews, Jr.)

The Third Sector: New Tactics for a Responsive Society (1973)

Marketing for Business Growth (1974)

The Marketing Imagination

Theodore Levitt

THE FREE PRESS
A Division of Macmillan, Inc.
NEW YORK

Collier Macmillan Publishers
LONDON

The Free Press
A Division of Macmillan, Inc.
866 Third Avenue, New York, N.Y. 10022

Collier Macmillan Canada, Inc.

Printed in the United States of America

printing number

5   6   7   8   9   10

Library of Congress Cataloging in Publication Data

Levitt, Theodore
  The marketing imagination.

  Includes index.
  1. Marketing.   I. Title.
HF5415.L482   1983   658.8   83-47989
ISBN 0-02-918840-7

CREDITS

With many thanks to Rachael Daitch,
more than a secretary

Contents

Preface

What's new? By this question people who manage mean, What unnoticed things "out there" can help or might hurt my business or my career, can create opportunities or impose perils? They also mean, What new techniques, new ways of doing things, can help us better do our jobs?

Those who answer professionally, with neatly engineered formulas, elegant strategic paradigms, and finely honed analytical techniques are sure to get an audience in this world of great uncertainty, profound ambiguity, and intense competition. Thus the ubiquity of shamans in business dress.

No manager with a detectable heartbeat does not periodically wonder, What's new?, does not wish for swift and magical solutions to troubling problems, for quick alleviation of daily distresses and the risks of uncertain futures. Managers are enormously vulnerable to the confident claims and plausible promises of outsiders peddling answers.

The uncertainties that concern managers most occur mostly in the market place, whether in the United States, the U.S.S.R., the United Arab Emirates, or the United Way. The market is palpable and inescapable. In its implacable operations the fates of all institutions are finally forged.

But the market place is not autonomous. It merely reflects the results of those who act upon it: those who "buy" in it and those who "sell" in it. They marshal materials, technologies, people, sentiments, wits, and money to their intended ends, meeting head-on in an amalgamating and unforgiving crucible.

The Marketing Imagination reflects the conviction that the way to deal with "what's new," as well as what's old and enduring, is mostly by being widely informed and thinking straight. Picking easy formulas or exotic models out of textbooks or other people's heads may be convenient and even occasionally helpful, but it does nothing for your mind or for your ability to deal effectively with the constantly emerging new realities. To "think straight" successfully in a world full of smart, straight-thinking people requires thinking with a special quality, transcending the ordinary and thus reaching imaginatively beyond the obvious or merely deductive. The future belongs to those who see possibilities before they become obvious and who effectively marshal resources and energies for their attainment or avoidance. Nor is anything great ever accomplished without high spirits.

The purpose of a business is to get and keep a customer. Without solvent customers in some reasonable proportion, there is no business. Customers are constantly presented with lots of options to help them solve their problems. They don't buy things, they buy solutions to problems. The surviving and thriving business is a business that constantly seeks better ways to help people solve their problems—functionally better, valued better, and available better. To create betterness requires knowing what customers think betterness to be. This precedes all else in business. The imagination that figures out what that is, imaginatively figures out what should be done, and does it with imagination and high spirits will drive the enterprise forward.

This book continues the stream of work of my most recent prior book, *Marketing for Business Growth* (1974). The chapters in this new book do not presume to tell people *how* to think straight or imaginatively. They simply deal with certain important matters in ways that textbooks, how-to books, and most professors and consultants generally do not. These ways apply to all types of businesses and to all other enterprises.

Chapter 1, "Marketing and the Corporate Purpose," sets the tone. It asserts what I've just said. "Profit" is a meaningless statement of the corporate purpose. Without customers in sufficient and steady numbers there is no business and no profit. No business can function effectively without a clear view of how to get customers, what its prospective customers want and need, and what options competitors give them, and without explicit strategies and programs focused on what goes on in the market place rather than on what's possible in the factory or what is merely assumed at headquarters. A chief executive who does not himself have a sense of the marketing requisites of his business or who does not have chief lieutenants who do is almost certainly headed for disaster. Marketing is, indeed, everybody's business, and everybody had better know it, no matter how deeply buried one may be in faraway R&D or out at the telephone switchboard.

Chapter 2, "The Globalization of Markets," asserts that the traditional multinational corporation is obsolete. It operates just as its name implies, multinationally, not globally. The future belongs to the globally, not multinationally, oriented corporation, because the globe is being homogenized by "The Republic of Technology." More and more, people everywhere are growing more alike in their wants and behavior, whether we're talking about Coca-Cola, microprocessors, jeans, movies, pizza, cosmetics, or milling machines. This means that the world explodes into a gigantic market in place of what used to be thought of as small segments or uniquely national markets. This will make even the smallest company in the smallest town subject to the ravages of global competition—competition based heavily on price. That's the new reality.

Chapter 3 is on "The Industrialization of Service." It asserts that ancient ideas about service are indeed ancient, being now replaced by industrial systems that make service both more efficient and more capable of being carried on in large scale that can be managed professionally and rationally, just like large manufacturing firms. Mom-and-pop services systems (in food, law, banking, repair, maintenance, and the like) will survive, but only just barely. The large, rationally managed service corporation is the new colossus that now affects us all—and all for the better. It takes a new kind of manager and management process.

Chapter 4 is called "Differentiation—of Anything." It asserts that differentiation is the essence of competition; that everything can be and is differentiable, even such "commodities" as steel, cement, money, chemicals, and grain. Success goes to those who differentiate themselves in ways that attract differentiably superior numbers of customers to themselves. It is, in fact, relatively easy to do. The point is to know how, and the chapter tells how, giving examples of how it's been successfully done.

Chapter 5, "Marketing Intangible Products and Product Intangibles," carries on some of the notions of Chapter 4, but with specific reference to what's usually called "service." The fact is, "service" is a central part of even the most massively durable tangible products, like earth-moving machines or a ton of stainless steel. All products have aspects of the tangible and the intangible. To know what these are and how to enhance and manage them gives differential competitive power to those who have this knowledge and do things right.

Chapter 6, on "Relationship Management," asserts that when you have a customer you have, in effect, an asset. That asset has to be managed lest the equity you have in that account be dissipated, lest the customer wonder, "What have you done for me lately?" This is particularly true as more of the world's work is done through long-term contracts or via supplier–customer links that must, of necessity, stretch out over many years. To manage the relationship that inevitably exists requires special care lest the equity in the account be destroyed, lest it decline to the point of vulnerability to a competitor's claims that "We can do more."

Chapter 7, "The Marketing Imagination," shows with specific illustrations much of what's been suggested in the preceding chapters. No amount of modern marketing science or heavy analysis will work without the protean powers of the marketing imagination and high spirits. The world looks for easy fixes and finely engineered programs to solve its problems. So also, these days, do people who manage. That's understandable. But this is a world of hungry and eager competitors constantly thinking up new things to do and new ways to do them, leapfrogging over the present, end-running around the powerfully entrenched. Their imagination is at work, and so must be the imaginations of those strongly established enterprises that got where they are largely via the imagination and enterprise of their managerial predecessors.

My expectation is that the reader will find in these and the remaining chapters much that can be put to immediate beneficial use. My greater *hope* is that the reader's cognitive system will somehow be positively affected, that the reader's marketing imagination will be strongly stimulated and will, as a result, continue to develop and yield great results.

My colleague Professor Abraham Zaleznik, a wise man about many things and modestly professing little knowledge of marketing, said casually one day, "What really drives your field is the marketing imagination." Hence the title.

THEODORE LEVITT
Harvard Business School

The
Marketing
Imagination

1

Marketing and the Corporate Purpose

Nothing in business is so remarkable as the conflicting variety of success formulas offered by its numerous practitioners and professors. And if, in the case of practitioners, they're not exactly "formulas," they are explanations of "how we did it," implying with firm control over any fleeting tendencies toward modesty that "that's how *you* ought to do it." Practitioners, filled with pride and money, turn themselves into prescriptive philosophers, filled mostly with hot air.

Professors, on the other hand, know better than to deal merely in explanations. We traffic instead in higher goods, like "analysis," "concepts," and "theories." In short, "truth." Filled with self-importance, we turn ourselves hopefully into wanted advisers, consultants filled mostly with woolly congestion.

I do not wish to disparage either, but only to suggest that these two legitimately different and respectable professions usually diminish rather than enhance their reputations when intruding too much or with too little thought on each other's turf.

How often have we heard executives of venerable age and high repute or entrepreneurs flushed with recent wealth pronounce with lofty certainty and imperial rectitude exactly what produces business success? All they really tell, however, in cleaned-up retrospection, is the story of how they themselves happen to have done it. Listen to ten, and you'll generally get ten different pieces of advice.

Listen to ten professors, and you'll generally get advice by some multiple of ten. The difference is not that professors believe more firmly in abundance. Rather, besides teaching, professors are also paid to think. Hence, lacking direct experience, each is likely to think up several different ways to get to the same place. People of affairs are paid merely to get there, and it is almost certain that when they do they'll think the only way there is the one they have taken, even when their neighbors got there by a different route.

On this score, people of affairs are scarcely unique. Consider the many versions we have heard from successful novelists of the "right way" to work: Sit down and get started, don't wait for inspiration; write when you're ready, not when the schedule says so; write from dawn till noon; write from dusk till dawn; always write in the same place; never stick to the same place for long; write only about what you know, don't invent; only invent, all else is mere confusion. The expert at doing things, obviously, is not reliably expert in either understanding what he does or why it works, certainly not in giving consistently good advice.

As a certified academic who is paid, however paltry the sum, to think, teach, and advise about the practices of those in practical work, of one thing I am totally convinced: the healthy state of business practice in the capitalist democracies. The state of business practice reflects the quality of the executive mind and its effective commitment to the purposes of business itself.

The modern executive mind is in very good condition indeed, especially in the larger and, usually therefore, global corporations. Indeed, awed admiration is what any intelligent and fair-minded analyst will come away with when he studies the large corporation of our times. For he will note its extraordinary efficiency, flexibility, agility, and internal diversity; the dedication and remarkable good spirits of its vast variety of employees; its attention to quality in what it does and to fairness in how it behaves; and the studiousness with which it approaches major undertakings. Notwithstanding all the self-righteousness parading of unpleasant contrary facts these days, no institution of any size or diversity, whether government or private, taking any reasonable combination of desirable attributes, can come anywhere near the large corporations of the modern capitalist democracies. Nor is this merely a matter of their having a head start historically. *Fortune*'s list of "Top 500" U.S. manufacturing corporations changes constantly, as does the list of top financial institutions. Federal Trade Commission studies of "industrial concentration" repeatedly show shifting patterns of leadership in one industry sector after another.

Obviously, being ahead or having gotten a head start counts for not a lot within America's little corner of the capitalist world. But the parallel fact that everywhere the capitalist corporations, as a group, are widening their lead over their lagging imitators in the noncapitalist world is extraordinarily significant. It means that being capitalistic gives them a genetic edge. Capitalism simply works better, and anybody who argues the opposite does just that. He argues. He simply doesn't have the facts.

One of the most interesting of these facts is that those who seek to catch up with the more advanced and achieving institutions of our times invariably seek to do it by some sort of selective imitation of the modern capitalist corporations. ("We'll take your best and ignore the rest.") Traffic in the opposite direction is negligible or nonexistent. Nothing could be more unmistakably meaningful. Nothing is more flattering to capitalism's protean prowess.

Even where this imitation now has a long history, having been generously helped with facilitating patents, designs, machines, control systems, technicians-on-loan, cash, whole factories supplied by the capitalist corporations—as they have

3

been in Soviet Russia ever since Lenin's New Economic Policy first imported Henry Ford in 1923—even when helped with the latest methods and technologies, the beneficiaries quickly fall behind again into inefficiency, sloth, and irrelevance. Why, one must ask, after more than half a century of eager (if grudging) imitation and gifts of capitalist technologies in the factories and on the farms have the Soviets fallen with uncomprehending frustration ever farther behind? Even their much-vaunted advanced fighter plane recently defected to Japan turned out to be advanced only in its packaging. At least they learned *that* much from us—the importance of packaging. This constant failure of helpful imitation to take hold persists also in nations with feudal military dictatorships and in the false democracies of South America, Southeast Asia, and now deimperialized Africa.

By what magic do the large corporations of the capitalist democracies work so well? Is it simply that they're capitalist, that they operate in democratic political environments, or some combination of the two? Or what?

The combination is crucial, emphatically. Being capitalist means the liberating absence of the feudal incubus, traditions that fetter people to their assigned masters rather than to their own chosen purposes. Operating in political democracies means the likelihood of public resistance to constantly advancing governmentalization of society, some reasonable probabilities against a constantly expanding and suffocating bureaucratization of the entire polity. (It is instructive, I think, to note that no dictatorship or tyranny has ever been voted in by people. People, however humble, however limited their education, quite naturally and sensibly resist Caesarism, however elegantly it may be packaged or differently presented.)

Nor is it any more presumed to be a reactionary cliché to say these things, as it once was in Western liberal intellectual circles. The cliché has now become the dismal, tragic truth. The firm belief, held by generations of intelligent and informed idealists, that justice and equality could be wedded through the ministrations of public servants working with diligent selflessness at control central has come a cropper. It's now obvious that the

4

future simply has not worked—not for Robert Owen, Karl Marx, Rosa Luxemburg, Sydney and Beatrice Webb, Rexford Guy Tugwell, or Oscar Lange, not even for Fidel Castro or Lyndon Baines Johnson.

What seems somehow to work best is something we call private enterprise and the free market system of economic organization operating in a political environment we call "representative democracy."

Unfortunately, this explanation is not the whole of it. Although, as we have seen, business enterprises in the modern capitalist democracies as a group outperform all other such enterprises operating under different conditions of political and economic organization, we also have seen that the distribution of this superiority is not symmetrical. Some firms prosper more than others. Some lag, wither, and even die. As I've suggested, the explanations of the superior performance that we commonly get from the most successful practitioners of capitalist enterprise, though perhaps quite accurate in themselves, are seldom more than confessions of particular experiences, offering no comparison with the experiences of others and devoid of serious analytical content. What they lack, moreover, in generality they often compensate with pomposity.

Professors also know something of the ways of pomposity, especially in the line of literary obfuscation masquerading as wisdom. They have dispensed some genuine wisdom as well, particularly about the special reasons why fairly free capitalist enterprises operating in relatively open markets vary in performance and about the characteristics associated with varying degrees of failure and success. That wisdom is, in fact, of relatively recent origin. Essentially it sets forth no more than the following few simple statements about the requisites of competitive success:

1. The purpose of a business is to create and keep a customer.
2. To do that you have to produce and deliver goods and services that people want and value at prices and under

5

conditions that are reasonably attractive relative to those offered by others to a proportion of customers large enough to make those prices and conditions possible.

3. To continue to do that, the enterprise must produce revenue in excess of costs in sufficient quantity and with sufficient regularity to attract and hold investors in the enterprise, and must keep at least abreast and sometimes ahead of competitive offerings.

4. No enterprise, no matter how small, can do any of this by mere instinct or accident. It has to clarify its purposes, strategies, and plans, and the larger the enterprise the greater the necessity that these be clearly written down, clearly communicated, and frequently reviewed by the senior members of the enterprise.

5. In all cases there must be an appropriate system of rewards, audits, and controls to assure that what's intended gets properly done and, when not, that it gets quickly rectified.

Not so long ago a lot of companies assumed something quite different about the purpose of a business. They said quite simply that the purpose is to make money. But that proved as vacuous as saying that the purpose of life is to eat. Eating is a requisite, not a purpose of life. Without eating, life stops. Profits are a requisite of business. Without profits, business stops. Like food for the body, profit for the business must be defined as the excess of what comes in over what goes out. In business it's called positive cash flow. It has to be positive, because the process of sustaining life is a process of destroying life. To sustain life, a business must produce goods and services that people in sufficient numbers will want to buy at adequate prices. Since production wears out the machinery that produces and the people who run and manage the machines, to keep the business going there's got to be enough left over to replace what's being worn out. That "enough" is profit, no matter what the accountants, the IRS, or the Gosplan calls it. *That* is why profit is a requisite, not a purpose of business.

Besides all that, to say that profit is a purpose of business

6

is, simply, morally shallow. Who with a palpable heartbeat and minimal sensibilities will go to the mat for the right of somebody to earn a profit for its own sake? If no greater purpose can be discerned or justified, business cannot morally justify its existence. It's a repugnant idea, an idea whose time has gone.

Finally, it's an empty idea. Profits can be made in lots of devious and transient ways. For people of affairs, a statement of purpose should provide guidance to the management of their affairs. To say that they should attract and hold customers forces facing the necessity of figuring out what people really want and value, and then catering to those wants and values. It provides specific guidance and has moral merit.

Something over twenty years ago this new way of thinking about business purposes led the more enlightened businesses slowly to distinguish operationally between marketing and selling, just as they now also distinguish between budgeting and planning, between long-range planning and strategic planning, between personnel management and human resources planning, between accounting and finance, between profit and cash flow, between the expected rate of return on investment and the present value of that expected rate of return.

All these are remarkably recent notions, few more than a generation old, developed mostly in our own lifetime. The most effective enterprises tend generally to practice them most conscientiously. They make a difference.

But of all these, the most powerful is the idea of marketing and the marketing view of the business process: that the purpose of a business is to create and keep a customer. There can be no corporate strategy that is not in some fundamental fashion a marketing strategy, no purpose that does not respond somehow to what people are willing to buy for a price. An asset consists of its capacity to generate revenue, either directly by its sale or by the sale of what it helps, finally, to produce. Even a quick, opportunistic raid on Wall Street has an underlying marketing rationale: that there's unrecognized or potential value greater than the value currently seen by others. The value is the asset, and that consists of its revenue-generating capability.

Indeed, those who usually consider themselves farthest re-

7

moved from the unsavory business of sales and marketing are often its most ardent practitioners. One need only to observe the constant competitive jockeying among Wall Street firms to determine exactly where their names will appear on the printed syndication lists of underwritings. Why, if not for its future revenue-producing value, does so much genteel intrigue occupy the time of such self-consciously proper investment bankers? Even more telling is the Wall Street assumption about the importance of flattery and obsequiousness in its relations with gigantic corporate customers. Special brass-plated, unnumbered side doors quietly admit the impressionable bigwigs with especially sought-after investment banking accounts. Heavily starched linen tablecloths, Waterford crystal, and imported chefs once apprenticed to Paul Bocuse characterize the opulent private dining rooms from which clients and prospective clients may enjoy spectacular views of the bustling city far down below. The packaging in which investment banking firms present themselves to their clients gets all the concentrated care that goes into packaging such other comparably hustled products as toiletries for the teeming masses.

Both practices endure because both work. Both customers buy hopeful expectations, not actual things. The ability to satisfy those expectations is more effectively communicated by the packaging than by simple generic description of what's in the package. Feelings are more important than feeling. How we feel about a car is more important than how the car feels. And so it should be, especially when we consider that in the most important decisions of life, like marriage, for example, we mostly decide on the basis of not the cold figures in our intended's balance sheet but our warm feelings about our intended's figure.

There is, however, a problem. In my 1960 manifesto, "Marketing Myopia," [1] marketing was elevated to a kind of corporate consciousness-raising. It asserted the intentionally narrow proposition that all energies should be directed toward satisfying the consumer, no matter what. The rest, given reasonable good

---

[1] Published in the *Harvard Business Review,* July/August 1960.

sense, would take care of itself. Nine years later, the manifesto having done its intended work, I offered a more conciliatory and sensible proposition: "The Marketing Matrix."[2] It incorporated some of the more broadly based wisdom about the corporate purpose that I've implied here, specifically, the need to balance, at some acceptable level of risk, the conditions of the external environment (customers, competition, government, and society) with the conditions of the internal environment (resources, competences, options, and wishes).

In "The Marketing Matrix," I asserted that early decline and certain death are the fate of companies whose policies are geared totally and obsessively to their own convenience at the total expense of the customer. The last of some twenty-five criteria offered to describe such companies was: "In setting your company goals, always set the standard in terms of production volume, revenues, profits, and expanded stockholder equity. Never state them also in terms of market factors, customer-need fulfillment, customer-service objectives, or market targets." In the matrix, the first part of this quoted example rated the top ranking of 9 on a nine-point scale of policies oriented entirely to the convenience of the company. The second part of this quoted example ("Never state them also in terms of market factors, customer need fulfillment" etc.) ranked a minimal 1 on a nine-point scale of policies oriented to the customer. This statement described, in short, a "9,1" company. There were examples also of "1,9" companies, "5,5" companies, and "9,9" companies. (The last were hard to find and as hard to imagine. Nobody can be *that* virtuous, not even under expert professorial guidance.)

The problem with the marketing concept was half-suggested in my chapter, "The Limits of the Marketing Concept," which followed directly after the matrix chapter. I am now about to drop the other shoe and suggest the remaining half of what is wrong with it. . . .

---

[2] Theodore Levitt, *The Marketing Mode* (New York: McGraw-Hill, 1969), Chap. 11, pp. 203–17.

9

In November 1976 IBM finally unveiled its first venture into the world of minicomputers—officially called Series/1. It did precisely what "Marketing Myopia" said it should: If customers prefer something that competes with your own offering, it is far more sensible for you to give it to them than to let competitors do it. It's better to participate in the destruction of your own market than to let it all be done by others. "Creative destruction," I called it, stealing that ringing phrase from Joseph Schumpeter, who was safely in the grave.

IBM was not the first company to enter the commercial computer business. It was, in fact, a particularly late latecomer. But in what seemed like no time, it captured at least 80 percent of the mainframe segment of what in 1976 was a $20 billion industry. It did so largely by being a singularly dedicated and spectacularly effective marketing company. Right through 1976, in its entire history this master symbol of modern science and technology had never had more than two senior executives who had not come up the organizational ladder primarily via the marketing route; and in that entire history, only one was a scientist. The master symbol of twentieth-century science and technology succeeded largely because of its marketing prowess, claims for the singular advantage imparted by the Forrester memory drum notwithstanding. It had industry managers who developed marketing plans, sales programs, and sales training for specifically targeted industries and companies in them. Its salesmen were as specialized in the industries to which they were assigned to sell as in the hardware they offered for sale. It bundled the software right into the product offering at a single set price, so that the customer was assured that the equipment would indeed be programmed to do the promised job. It designated installation facilities for the customer, redesigned his entire data collection and reporting systems, trained his data processing people, took the shakedown cruise, and then later developed new EDP applications to help the client even more. In the process the client became an even bigger and more dependent customer. Meanwhile the customer had the option of paying the single nonnegotiable price either by paying outright for everything or by leasing it with virtually no punitive cancellation provisions. If ever there was a thoroughgoing marketing-oriented professional organization, it was IBM. And it worked like magic.

But in November 1976, with Series/1, all that was chucked. The sales force was made product-oriented rather than customer- and application-oriented. It became a dedicated sales force, dedicated to selling Series/1 hardware, and that's it. No special customer help. Sell, sell, sell to everybody on the landscape. And no more leasing options. Cash on the barrelhead, that's all, in spite of the fact that IBM's easy financial capability of offering the lease option had long given it a powerful competitive edge.

Series/1 is clearly a case of creative destruction—competing with yourself in order to save yourself. Nothing is really new about that. But abandoning marketing, sales, and pricing practices that had proved so effective for almost totally opposite practices, *that's* new.

That same week in November 1976 *Business Week's* lead article on Revlon, Inc., had the following headline and subhead: "Management Realists in the Glamour World of Cosmetics: Flair and flamboyance yield to controls, budgets, planning." We all know enough to guess from that what was in the article. We should also know that in the first year of an entirely new operating style, one that substituted management for mystique, sales rose 18 percent and profits 16 percent. Nine months into the next year sales were up another 23 percent and earnings 25 percent.

Just as successful managers and entrepreneurs who presume to give advice to all others on the basis of their own limited experiences are likely to give advice of limited relevance or utility, so do professors of business administration when their ideas become as rigid as other people's experiences. Series/1 switched to product-orientedness because conditions changed. In the Series/2 family (which was sure to come), customer- and application-orientedness once again became competitively appropriate. Likewise, who is to say that Revlon, no matter how

11

big it gets, will be able always to function effectively and prosperously under its new managerial dispensation? Maybe for some purposes miscegenation will become the mode. In the words of Richard Barrie, the new president of Faberge Inc., "Somewhere along the line the industry has to shake off the old idea of management by mystique, yet still retain the mystique in its marketing." Who's to say?

The world of competitive enterprises openly facing each other in open markets is clearly a world of constant change. The marketing concept alerts us to this fact with the prescriptive injunction that to keep up requires studying and responding to what people want and value, and quickly adjusting to choices provided by competitors. It alerts us especially to the fact that competition often comes from outside the industry in which it finally occurs. Deeply implanted in these ideas is the notion that nothing is more important than the customer. The customer is, once more, King.

Suddenly IBM said in 1976 something that appeared quite different: "Be product-, not customer-oriented." Revlon appears to say, "Run the company, don't just run after the customer." And they're both obviously right. Being a "1,9" company (little company-oriented, highly customer-oriented) doesn't really work. Nor does being a "9,1" company. "9,9" is probably impossible, and "5,5" is probably an invitation to get outflanked on all sides.

The problem with the marketing concept, like all concepts in business, "laws" in physics, theories in economics, and all philosophies and ideologies, is a persistent tendency toward rigidity. They get dogmatized, interpreted into constantly narrower and inflexible prescriptions. In the case of the marketing concept, this is especially dangerous because of marketing's centrality in shaping the purposes, strategies, and tactics of the entire organization.

There is not, and cannot be, any rigid and lasting interpretation of what the marketing concept means in the specific ways a company should operate at any given time. Consider the cases of IBM and Revlon once again, and others.

IBM

In Series/1, as in its original entry into the computer business, the company was an imitator, a follower of others that preceded it by many years into the market with the product. But when the computer was a relatively new idea, its manufacturers knew a great deal more about its potential uses and usability than its potential users. The needs of potential users for the product had to be converted into wants. For wants to become purchases, the purchasers had to be carefully educated and guided to the product's uses. IBM had to educate its own sales people in the businesses to which they were to sell. All this was not so different from the creation of a mass market for eye shadow and eye liners just a decade ago. The big cosmetics houses had to establish demonstration counters in the stores to teach women how to use the product.

But once educated, either by the seller or by the mushrooming number of independent schools and courses available elsewhere as the markets expanded, the customer became able to make his own decisions about what he needed and how to use it. Thus the more successful the sellers became in teaching their prospects to want and use their products, the less dependent their users became on their sellers. In the first instance, "the product" being sold was a complex cluster of value satisfactions that included education, training, hands-on help, continuing advice, and quick availability for emergency situations. Later, in maturity, as the customer became more sophisticated, "the product" by definition became much simpler. It became, if not exactly a commodity, certainly not a complex cluster of things. It became, simply, a computer; simply an elegant little dish of eye shadow.

But more. As the computer got involved in more things in the corporation (largely at first with the suggested help of its manufacturers, and later more and more with the help of internal specialists in the user organization), it became a hard-to-manage monster. Different users within the organization made different and often conflicting demands on it. It became a continuing battle as to how to charge different departments and individuals for its use and for the accompanying software, which proved increasingly costly. All this finally created a market for the mini-computer. A corporate department, division, or even individual could now have his own small computer, programmed or programmable the way he wanted it. The invention of integrated circuits and then microprocessors turned a trickle into a flood.

With customers as sophisticated about the product as its sellers, with equipment costs low, and with strongly established competing sellers, the properly marketing-oriented thing for IBM to have done was precisely what it did: sell the simple hardware hard, without the attendant beneficiating clusters of the past. And it worked, like magic, just as did the personal computer a few years later.

Revlon

As one finally lays down Andrew Tobias's book about the bizarre, coruscating career of Charles Revson, *Fire and Ice: The Story of Charles Revson, The Man Who Built the Revlon Empire,*[1] it is clear enough that toward the end Revson himself began to wonder about the fickle feudal terror with which he ran his empire. His escalating ad hominum hatred of his competitors merely mirrored his uncertainties about his managerial methods. When finally, after several shatteringly disastrous trials with managers of a different breed, he bought Michel C. Bergerac, the elegant French-born head of International Telephone and Telegraph Corporation's European operations, he set into motion at Revlon precisely the same kind of transformation that characterized Series/1. So urgently did Revson feel the need that he paid Bergerac $1.5 million just for signing up with Revlon, added a five-year contract for a salary of $325,000 a year, and three-year options for 70,000 shares of stock.

The problem was that competition had become more professionalized, with some of the biggest cosmetics houses having

[1] New York: Morrow, 1976.

been sold to drug and package-goods companies. The regulatory climate had become tougher. Distribution costs suddenly rose sharply, with competition making it harder to get compensating price rises. The tonnage of what moved out the factory gates suddenly became as crucial as the tone of its colors. Bergerac, whose Continental suaveness assuaged Revlon's hard-eyed glamour merchants, also earned their respect for his ITT management methods. No longer did the merchandising tail so vigorously wag the management dog—things were just as they should be. And it worked, like magic, more recent setbacks not withstanding.

Allegheny Ludlum Steel

Not so long ago stainless steel was a specialty steel. As with computers, customers had to be created by being taught and shown how to use it and what might be done to use it more abundantly to give them as well a competitive edge in *their* markets. The most important part of "the product" in those early days was not the steel itself but the design and application services provided by its chief manufacturer, Allegheny Ludlum Steel. Customers who were buying regular carbon steel, often more conveniently and in smaller quantities and with faster deliveries from local independent steel warehouses, now bought stainless steel quite willingly from the factory in larger quantities, with longer delivery times and no price shadings. They needed the factory's help on other matters more than the local warehouses' convenience.

In time, however, the independent warehouse market share of stainless steel rose. Allegheny Ludlum lost market share to competitors who sold more intensively through such warehouses. As in IBM's case, the customer, having been educated, no longer needed the supplier's attendant cluster of benefits— or, at least, needed less of them. Selling had to become less marketing-oriented, in the traditional sense, and more vigorously product- and sales-oriented. The number of warehouses had to be expanded or mill inventories expanded so as to speed up deliveries. In selling, "who you know" became relatively more important than "what you know."

Allegheny Ludlum changed to a new mode. It cannot be said that it scuttled the marketing concept. Instead it adopted a new version, a new marketing mode to deal with different needs and pressures. It did not ignore the customer, did not try to shove down his throat what he did not want. It merely simplified and streamlined "the product" to the customer's new specifications. The marketing concept remained in healthy charge, only now it called for something different from what was becoming, in some places, a rigidly dogmatized version of what it should be. And it worked, like magic.

Chevrolet

Take, on the other hand, Chevrolet at General Motors. To read Alfred P. Sloan Jr.'s autobiographical *My Years with General Motors,* the advice one walks away with about running a successful company includes the idea that each item in the corporate product line should have a clearly distinctive identity, even though all the products are generically the same. "A car is a car," but not really. A Chevrolet was actually a low-priced entrée car, built for youthful peppiness yet roomy enough for new-family practicality. Next came the Pontiac step-up, a clear rise on the ladder of its owner's maturity and success. The larger, sturdier, more impressive Buick was for the solidly achieving middle manager, solidly on the road to better things. The Oldsmobile confirmed the attainment of those better things, and the Cadillac of the best things. Everybody knew clearly whom the car was for and exactly what its possession signified.

But for nearly two decades Chevrolet has now successfully violated Sloan's sacred dicta. Its *own* line of cars is itself wider than the entire General Motors line during Sloan's remarkably successful tenure as its chief executive officer. Not only is it wider in the sizes and prices of its cars and the options it offers the customers for them, but it even has more brand names of its own than Sloan ever had for the entire corporation. Meanwhile, all General Motors divisions have expanded their lines (up and down) across each other's turfs, and still the Chevrolet division prospers more than ever, as does the entire corporation. And there's not the slightest whiff of evidence that it's a fragile castle built up momentarily out of sand.

Only a fool would argue that Chevrolet is not market-oriented or that General Motors is confused or has gone berserk. Certainly Alfred Sloan would approve, though his book implies the opposite. His book was written for times when cars were more important as symbols of attainment or expressions of as-pirations. As the customer has changed, so has General Motors. And it's worked, like magic. Now even General Motors is pro-posing joint-venture production of subcompacts with Toyota. More magic.

Exxon/Gulf

Finally, contrast Exxon and Gulf in the late 1950s for final proof that not even the luck of sudden riches from beneath the Arabian sands can save one from the necessity of doing things right. Gulf, at that time the biggest beneficiary of all, opted for quick conversion of oil into cash. It vastly expanded its service station network throughout the United States, leasing new lands for grand new stations and, just as fast, leasing marginal old stations in declining places. It even created a subregular grade of gasoline, Gulftane, to be sold along with regular and supreme for a penny less than regular.

Exxon opted for the opposite. It stuck to a policy of careful new-site selection and systematic elimination of older and de-clining stations. It began to buy the land and buildings of its service stations, thus balancing one type of expanding fixed asset in distant lands with another type "at home" where land values were on a secular rise. Moreover, owning rather than leasing its retail outlets made it easier to modify them to the specifications with which it sought to attract more customers per outlet. It worked harder at selecting and training its service station attendants. And though, like Gulf, it acquired lots more stations, it did so by buying not individual stations but entire companies that were specifically in the retail gasoline vending business. These Exxon upgraded and gradually shifted over to its own brand.

Long before October 1973, when suddenly oil-in-the-ground nearly quadrupled in value, and even before increasing ownership participations and expropriations by the Arab countries had reduced the share of what was physically left in the ground, it became apparent to Gulf that it had made a major error. It proved more costly to sell, in small and declining stations, gasoline made from cheap crude than to sell, in larger, more efficient ones, gasoline made from more costly crude. That discovery was foretold long before by others. But what proved more costly than these expenses alone was the attendant destruction of customers. In this case, as opposed to General Motors, expanding the line downward (Exxon expanded it upward, with a super-premium) and expanding the types of stations and locations produced confusion both within Gulf and among its customers. What little serious brand preference there is among major-brand gasoline buyers almost totally vanished for Gulf. With the greatest cost in money and human spirit within the corporation, Gulf for a decade now has been trying to undo and redo what it did so fast in just a few years before. In the 1950s it suddenly *did* become obsessively product-oriented. And it worked, like magic, in the wrong direction.

These examples tell us something we all know but don't always practice in our thoughts and actions: that to refer to an organization's principal marketing policies and strategies is to refer to that organization's principal overall corporate policies and strategies; its principal overall corporate policies and strategies cannot be shaped absent serious marketing considerations; that there are stages in the evolution of markets that may require policies and strategies that appear, falsely, to be perversely product-oriented; but in all this variation and adjustment and oscillation there must be persistent, remorseless, unforgiving, overriding orderliness and logic, no matter how much things seem to be different or to change. This overriding orderliness is the logic of the marketing concept. The market calls the tune, and the players had better play it right.

. . . When people of affairs in their twilight years presume to tell all others "how to do it" by telling merely how *they* happen to have done it, they may be right for their particular one day of the year but not necessarily for the remaining 364. It may be that it takes a Copernicus or a Kepler to study the entire whole in order for the rest of us to understand the underlying order, the constants that the daily pressures of events keep us from recognizing as constants. Down there in the competitive ring, things seldom look as panoramically clear as up in the stands where the observers sit in detached comfort.

But the fact that things can't be *seen* so well by those in the ring does not suggest that what they say is any less true. Certainly it will be more keenly felt. Nothing is as bracing or as certain as what is directly experienced. . . . The people of affairs, the practitioners out there who fight the bull, have fundamental wisdom. What they experience and feel in the difficult life of directing and managing organizations has to be respected. Only *they* know how it feels, but they know only how it feels in *their* particular circumstances and from the angle of vision provided them *down there* on the turf. Up here in the stands we know little of how it feels but perhaps a lot about how it looks, especially as compared with all the others down there on the turf. And from this comparison it is possible, though generally difficult, to know also what it means.

I see a constant that defines the best. It says that there can be no effective corporate strategy that is not marketing oriented, that does not in the end follow this unyielding prescript: The purpose of a business is to create and keep a customer. To do that, you have to do those things that will make people *want* to do business with you. All other truths on this subject are merely derivative.

2

The Globalization of Markets

A powerful force now drives the world toward a single converging commonality, and that force is technology. It has proletarianized communication, transport, and travel, making them easily and cheaply accessible to the world's most isolated places and impoverished multitudes. Suddenly no place and nobody is insulated from the alluring attractions of modernity. Almost everybody everywhere wants all the things they have heard about, seen, or experienced via the new technological facilitators that drive their wants and wishes. And it drives these increasingly into global commonality, thus homogenizing markets everywhere.

The result is a new commercial reality—the explosive emergence of global markets for globally standardized products, gigantic world-scale markets of previously unimagined magnitudes.

Corporations geared to this new reality generate enormous

economies of scale in production, distribution, marketing, and management. When they translate these into equivalently reduced world prices, they devastate competitors that still live functionally in the disabling grip of old assumptions about how the world now works.

The world's aspirations now level simultaneously outward and upward, with increasingly larger portions of its population greedily wanting the modernity to which they are so constantly exposed. This in part explains the spectacular and staggering external debts from which so many nations now desperately suffer—not just the somewhat developed ones like Mexico, Brazil, and Rumania, but also several dozen Third World ones like Togo and Malawi. Each for the past decade has raced with exuberant recklessness toward the acquisition of modernity it could not or would not discipline itself to afford, each driven by the urgent demands of its people for what they knew as the comforts and indulgences of people in the developed nations.

All parts of the world want the most advanced things that the most advanced sectors already have, and no longer will merely the same classes and types of goods and services satisfy them. They also want them in their most advanced states of functionality, quality, reliability, service levels, and price competitiveness. Gone are the days when you could sell in the less-developed world last year's models or the used equipment you took as trade-in at home. Gone are the days when you could count on attractive markets in smaller countries for lesser versions of the advanced products that enjoyed solid markets in the advanced countries. Gone are the days when prices, margins, and profits abroad were generally better than at home.

Gone too, or going rapidly, are the accustomed differences in national and regional preferences regarding product or service features. Now in all respects the world levels up in all places to world-standard commonality.

This means the end of the multinational commercial world, and with it the end of the multinational corporation. The new reality is the globalization of markets, and with it the powerful materialization of the global corporation.

Not every company with a presence in more than one nation professes to be multinational. But some that pretend or seem to be are not that at all. Where the purpose of occupancy in another land is merely to extract or even to process raw materials for use in the home country, the company cannot be sensibly though of as a multinational. To be meaningfully multinational, a company must have an operating presence in the markets of other nations. To be merely an extractor, processor, or buyer of nature's riches elsewhere for use and sale at home, no matter how gigantic or geographically dispersed these efforts might be, is to be merely a multinational buyer, not a multinational business. To be a multinational business requires an operating customer-getting presence of meaningful scale in a variety of national markets. The difference is on the order of that between an international tourist and a committed world citizen.

The multinational and the global corporation are not the same. The multinational corporation operates in a number of countries, where in each case it adjusts with accommodating care and therefore high relative costs to the presumptive special conditions of the particular country. In contrast, the global corporation operates with resolute constancy and therefore at low relative costs as if the entire world (or major regions of it) were a single, largely identical entity; it does and sells the same things in the same single way everywhere.

Which strategy is better is a matter not of opinion but of necessity. Widespread communication and travel pound the same constant drumbeat of modern possibilities into the human consciousness everywhere, particularly the possibilities to lighten and enhance work, to raise living standards, and to divert and entertain. Modernity is not only the wish but actually also the widespread practice, even among those who cling with philistine passion or religious fervor to ancient attitudes and heritages.

Who can forget during the worst of the 1979 Iranian uprisings the televised scenes of inflamed young men in fashionable French-cut trousers and silky body shirts open to the waist, with raised modern weapons, thirsting for blood in the name of Islamic fundamentalism?

In Brazil thousands of eager migrants from the preindustrial Bahian wilderness swarm daily into the exploding coastal cities, quickly to install television sets in crowded corrugated-iron huts before which, next to battered Volkswagens, they make sacrificial candlelight offerings of fruit and fresh-killed chickens to the Macumban spirits.

In the fratricidal war of extermination against the Ibos, daily television reports revealed, for all the world to see, soldiers in remote places, with bloodstained swords, listening to transistor radios and drinking Coca-Cola.

In the isolated Siberian city of Krasnoyarsk, absent of paved streets and uncontrolled news, occasional Western travelers are stealthily propositioned for their cigarettes, their digital watches, and even the clothes off their backs.

A thriving underground trade in modern weapons and military mercenaries reaches deeply into underdeveloped places, exceeded in magnitude only by organizing smuggling of electronic equipment, used automobiles, Western clothing, cosmetics, and pirated movies.

A thousand little suggestive scenes attest to the ubiquity of what is so clearly obvious in well-traveled places elsewhere: the rapid homogenization of the world's wants and wishes regarding the most advanced things the world makes and sells, and the ways in which these are made and sold. Daniel J. Boorstin, Librarian of Congress and author of the monumental trilogy, *The Americans,* has characterized our age as driven by "The Republic of Technology," whose "supreme law . . . is convergence, the tendency for everything to become more like everything else."

In business this has clearly translated into global markets, with global corporations selling the same single standardized products—autos, steel, chemicals, petroleum, cement, agricultural commodities and equipment, industrial and commercial construction, banking, insurance, computers, semiconductors, transport, electronic instruments, pharmaceuticals, and telecommunications, to mention only a few of the obvious—largely in the same single ways everywhere.

Nor is the sweeping gale of global competition confined

merely to so-called commodity or high-tech products, where standardization is facilitated by customers and users who speak the universal language of science and engineering. The transforming winds whipped up by proletarianized communication and travel enter every crevice of life everywhere. Boorstin wrote: "The converging forces of everyday experience [that 'The Republic of Technology' has ushered in] are both sublingual and translingual. People who never could have been persuaded to read Goethe will eagerly drive a Volkswagen. . . . Technology dilutes and dissolves ideology."

Commercially, nothing confirms this so much as the booming success of McDonald's everywhere from the Champs Elysees to the Ginza, of Coca-Cola in Bahrain and Pepsi in Moscow, and of rock music, Greek salad, Hollywood movies, Revlon cosmetics, Sony televisions, and Levi jeans everywhere. Thus "high-touch" products are as globalized as high-tech. Indeed, globalization goes even further. The Princeton sociologist Suzanne Keller notes that everywhere that's touched by industrialization and urbanization is characterized by rising divorce rates and two-paycheck marriages, declining birth rates, and a generation gap in sexual mores.

Both the high-tech and the high-touch ends of life's continuum merge into global commonality, gradually consuming the undistributed middle into the orbit of cosmopolitanism. Nothing is exempt, and nothing can stop it. Everywhere everything gets more like everything elese, as the world's preference structure gets pressed into homogenized commonality.

Ancient differences in national tastes and preferences, in modes of doing business and the institutions of commerce, fall before the homogenizing modernity everybody experiences via the new technological facilitators. The global commonality of what's preferred leads inescapably to the global standardization of products, of manufacturing, and of the institutions of trade and commerce. Small nation-based markets are transmogrified and expanded into large global-sized markets, with accompanying economies of scale in production, distribution, marketing, and management. This leads to growing world competition based on efficiency in production, distribution, marketing, and management. Inevitably this generates worldwide competitive intensity focused powerfully on price. With price therefore once again the dominant basis of world competition, the way to be the most effective price competitor is to incorporate superior quality and reliability into the price offering. This converges finally into world-standardized product lines that compete on the basis of appropriate value—the best combinations of price, quality, reliability, and delivery for products that, in respect to design, functionality, and even fashionability, are globally identical.

That, and little else, explains much of the surging success of such a vast variety of Japanese companies dealing in such a vast variety of products around the globe—both tangible products like steel, cars, motorcycles, hi-fi equipment, farm machinery, robots, microprocessors, carbon fibers, and now even textiles, and intangible products like banking, shipping, general contracting, and soon, certainly, computer software. Nor are high-quality and low-cost operations incompatible, as argued unanimously with vigorous vacuity for nearly twenty years until 1982 by varieties of data engineers and hustling consulting organizations. The reported data are incomplete, wrongly analyzed, and contradictory. "You can observe a lot just by watching," said Yogi Berra. To "observe" means to put your mind to what the eyes see. The observing mind apprehends everywhere that low-cost operations are the hallmark of superior managerial cultures whose superiority requires and produces superior quality in all that they do and touch. High quality and low cost are not opposing paths. They are the necessary compatible identities of superior practice.

To deny that Japan's case fits the definition of global practices with glib references to certain facts—that at home Japanese cars have right-side drives but they export left-side drives to the United States and the European Continent, that they will sell office machines through distributors in the United States but direct at home, that Japanese bankers speak Portuguese in Brazil, that in France Japanese products and packages are labeled in French—all this is to mistake a difference for a distinction. The steering wheel locations are different, and so are the distribution channels and the language. What is distinctive about Japan is the unrelenting drive for economizing and value-enhancing distinction. And that spells everywhere and in everything a drive for global standardization at high-quality levels.

The governing theory is that with reasonably restrained concern for suitability, if you force costs and prices down and push quality and reliability in all things up, everywhere around the world customers will prefer your world-standardized generic offerings in rising proportions, regardless of what conventional market research and even common observations may suggest about the existence of different national and intranational tastes, preferences, needs, and institutions. In this theory the Japanese have been repeatedly vindicated, as was Henry Ford with the Model T in his time. And they have been repeatedly copied with remarkable success by companies in South Korea (television sets and heavy construction), Malaysia (personal calculators and micro computers), Brazil (auto parts and tools), Colombia (apparel), Singapore (optical equipment), and yes, even in the United States (office copiers, computers, bicycles, castings), Western Europe (automatic washing machines), Rumania (housewares), Hungary (apparel), Yugoslavia (furniture), and Israel (pagination equipment).

Of course, not even large companies that operate only in a single nation or even in a single large city standardize everything they make, sell, or do within their chosen markets. That's why they have product lines, not just one single product version, and multiple distribution channels and the like. There are neighborhood, local, regional, ethnic, and institutional differences even within large cities. But all that is beside the point. Though companies always customize for specific segments, success in a world whose wants become more homogenized requires of such companies strategic and operating modes that search for opportunities to sell to similar segments throughout the globe to achieve the scale economies that keep their costs competitive.

Seldom these days is a segment in one country unique to that country alone. It is found everywhere, thus available to sellers from everywhere. Small local segments in this fashion become globally standardized, large, and therefore subject to global competition, especially price competition.

The globally oriented competitor will constantly seek opportunities to achieve global scale by globally standardizing everything he does in order to maintain his cost competitiveness. The otherwise globally oriented competitor who digresses from this mode does so at his peril, and only after having exhausted all possibilities of standardization while retaining good profitability with segmentation. Meanwhile, having digressed and diverged from standardization, he will push constantly for its reinstatement instead of drifting further into minuscule scale diseconomies.

This does not mean the end of choice or market segments. It means the beginning of price competition for quality products aimed at fewer but larger global market segments.

Increasingly in our homogenized world trouble will stalk the company that lacks a clarified global focus and is inattentive to the simple economics of simplicity and standardization. The most endangered companies are those that produce largely for, and dominate, relatively small domestic markets with high-value-added products for which there are small markets in all countries. With transportation low proportionately to their total costs, and in any case relatively cheap, competitors with global reach, with products produced more cheaply under modern scale-efficient conditions, will successfully enter the distant sheltered markets to which provincial producers have become complacently accustomed. This means the end of domestic territoriality—certainly for products with these characteristics. No matter how diminutive they may otherwise seem, the globe is their competitive crucible.

The new Republic of Technology homogenizes world tastes, wants, and possibilities into global-market proportions, which allows for world-standardized products, giving the global producer powerful scale advantages. When his lower costs are offered to the international multitudes, markets are expanded doubly, as previous holdouts for local preferences in product features, design, and functionality sacrifice these to the superior attractions of price alone. Thus the strategy of standardization not only responds to world homogenized markets but actually expands them with aggressively low prices.

In this way the new technological juggernaut taps into an ancient motivation: to make one's money go as far as possible. And that is something no one has ever suggested is anything but universal.

The difference between the hedgehog and the fox, in distinguishing between Dostoevski and Tolstoy, Sir Isaiah Berlin explained, is that the fox knows a lot about a great many things, but the hedgehog knows everything about one great thing. The multinational corporation knows a lot about a great many countries, and congenially adapts itself to their supposed differences. The global corporation knows one great thing about all countries, and lures them to its custom by capitalizing on the one great thing they all have in common. The global corporation looks to the nations of the world not for how they are different but for how they are alike. While it recognizes the presumed need to be globally competitive as well as nationally responsive, it seeks constantly in every way to standardize everything into a common global mode. And it does this, to repeat the point, by capitalizing on what, increasingly, is the one great thing all nations and people have in common.

The one great thing all nations and people have in common is scarcity. Nobody takes scarcity lying down. Everybody everywhere wants to get out of the inescapability of his insufficiency as much as possible. Everybody wants more. Even those blessedly gone hippies who sought, for a decade, escape in communal penury, proclaimed unctuously that "less is more." They too wanted more—their kind of more—in exchange for the scarcity they could not escape and would not abide.

Almost nowhere is anyone totally self-sufficient. Hence we have everywhere some sort of trade, barter, and money. Division of labor and specialization of production are the means by which people and nations optimize their benefits via trade, barter, and money. Experience teaches everyone the three special qualities of money: scarcity, difficulty of acquisition, and transcience. This explains the reluctance with which people part

28

with it and the care they exercise in doing so. It also explains part of the "one great thing" the global corporation knows: If you can get the price low enough, the increasingly homogenized world will increasingly take your world-standardized offering, even if it isn't exactly what your old mother said was suitable, what immemorial custom decreed as right, or what market-research fabulists asserted was preferred.

The implacable truth of all modern production—of tangible as well as intangible products—is that the more standardized product costs less than the less standardized product, and that the large-scale production of standardized products or components is generally cheaper within a wide range of volume than small-scale production. It is cheaper to do things one or two ways, rather than three, four, or five ways. Hence if the world is treated as one or two distinctive product markets, it can be more economically served than if it is treated as three, four, or five product markets. The global corporation strives to treat the world as fewer standardized markets rather than as many customized markets. It actively seeks and vigorously works toward global convergence. That is its real distinction. Modernity is its mission and price competition its mode, even when it sells top-of-the-line, high-priced products. By contrast, the multinational corporation willingly accepts obvious vestigial national differences, questioning not the possibilities of their transformation, recognizing not how the world is ready and even eager for the benefactions of modernity, especially when the price is right. The multinational corporation's accommodating mode to visible national differences is medieval, and so are its offerings and its prices.

As I have said, global convergence is not the special case of technologically and scientifically advanced products, of high-tech as opposed to high-touch. Consider once more the amazing cases of Coca-Cola and Pepsi-Cola, which by any conceivable criteria are globally standardized products sold globally with standardized communications, and welcomed eagerly by everybody everywhere. Most extraordinary is the fact that both are a product that is ingested through the mouth, crossing to everybody's satisfaction multitudes of taste buds trained immemorially to an enormous variety of preferred and deeply ingrained local differences as to flavor, consistency, effervescence, and aftertaste. Yet everywhere these two invariant products are successfully and expandingly sold in the same way. So too with cigarettes, especially American-made cigarettes, which make year-to-year inroads almost everywhere on hitherto powerful preferences for other tobacco blends. These are not special incidents. They are examples of the general drift toward world homogenization, even in high-touch products, of the means by which all products are distributed and financed, of the way they are priced, and of the institutions through which and the ways by which they are sold.[1] Nothing is exempt. The products and methods of the industrialized world play a single tune for all the world, and all the world eagerly dances to it.

The world moves inexorably forward to greater global convergence in all things, propelled by the technological forces that shape our times. Such differences as remain are vestiges of the hardened inherited past as to cultural preferences, national tastes and standards, and the institutions of business itself. Some yield gradually, while others actually themselves expand globally. That explains, for example, the growth of so-called ethnic markets the world over—specialty segments in foods, clothing, entertainment, and even retail institutions such as delicatessens, boulangeries, and antique shops. These are not denials or contradictions of global homogenization, but rather its confirmation. Without the generalized homogenization of tastes and preferences there would be no distinction in ethnicity or specialization. To have the latter requires the dominant presence of the former. The global growth of ethnic markets confirms the greater presence of global standardization in all else and is itself an example of the global standardization of segments. Everywhere there is Chinese food, pita bread, country and western music, pizza, and jazz. The global pervasiveness of

[1] In 1968 Robert D. Buzzell published a landmark article ("Can You Standardize Multinational Marketing?", *Harvard Business Review,* November/December 1968), in which he catalogued the conditions that facilitated and inhibited standardization. Regarding the latter, he pointed out, even then, the rapidity with which barriers to standardization were falling—and in all cases they fell to the better economics and alleviations of more advanced ways of doing things.

ethnic forms represents the cosmopolitanization of specialty segments. Again, globalization does not mean the end of segments. It means, instead, their expansion to worldwide proportions.

Vast differences in products and product features remain between different nations that have a heavy presence of multinational corporations. And there remain vast differences in how these corporations conduct business in those nations. But many of these differences merely reflect the respectful accommodation of multinational corporations to what they believe are fixed local preferences. They *believe* things are fixed not because they are, but because those who believe this have a fixed habit of thinking and acting multinationally rather than globally. They simply have not pressed at all, or have not pressed properly, for global standardization.

I do not mean to advocate systematic disregard of local or national differences. I maintain, rather, that sensitivity to them does not require one to ignore the possibilities of doing things differently or better. There are, for example, enormous differences among the Middle Eastern oil countries. Some are socialist, some monarchies, some republics. Some take their legal heritage from the Napoleonic Code, some from the Ottoman Empire, some from the British Common Law, and all are influenced by Islam. But in all, to do business there means to personalize the business relationship in an almost obsessively intimate fashion. It requires respecting national holidays, which means, during the Ramadan, a month of starting business discussions after ten o'clock at night, when people are tired and full of food. One almost never has the option of going without a local partner or co-venturer. A local lawyer is a must, as are irrevocable letters of credit. But, as Coca-Cola's Senior Vice President Sam Ayoub said recently, "Arabs are much more capable of making distinctions between cultural and religious purposes on the one hand and economic realities on the other than is generally assumed. Islam is compatible with science and modern times."[2]

Nor are barriers to modernity confined to countries such as these. There are legal and financial impediments to the free

[2] In a speech given in summer 1982 at Pebble Beach, California.

31

transfer of technology and data across the boundaries even of European Common Market countries. There is resistance to radio and television interference (i.e., "pollution") among proximate European countries. But the past is a good guide to the future on these matters—namely, that with persistence and appropriate means, in the past barriers against superior technologies and better economics have always fallen. It is very much a matter of time and effort.

Many companies that have made the effort tried to standardize world practice and tried to export wholesale, without accommodation or change, products and practices to other nations, and failed miserably in the process. Such failures have generally been seized upon as evidence of bovine stupidity in the face of abject impossibility. Advocates of the possibility of global standardization have used such failures as examples merely of failures of execution. The result is a standoff.

Still, poor execution explains many failed attempts to standardize world practices and products. Horror stories are abundant, too obvious to merit recitation for our education. What are far more instructive are stories of failures to conceive of the global possibilities, and more especially of failure of nerve.

Consider the case of fully automatic home laundry equipment in Western Europe at the time when few homes had even semi-automatic or even manual machines. Hoover, Ltd., with its parent company headquartered in North Canton, Ohio, and a long, prominent presence in England as a vacuum cleaner producer, had also established a strong presence there with its Hoover-branded washing machines, and to a lesser extent also with washers on the Continent. Its large washing machine plant in England operated uneconomically far below capacity, with little possibility of filling it with production for the U.K. market alone. It needed substantially greater sales on the Continent for either its semi-automatic or its fully automatic machines. Thinking itself properly market-oriented, it conducted carefully professional competitive and consumer-preference studies in Great Britain and in each of the major Continental countries. The research proved clearly enough, as Exhibit 1 shows, what product features were preferred in each country.

EXHIBIT 1. CONSUMER PREFERENCES AS TO AUTOMATIC WASHING MACHINE FEATURES, BY COUNTRY

Features	United Kingdom	Italy	Germany	France	Sweden
Shell dimensions[1]	34″ & narrow	Low & narrow	34″ & wide	34″ & narrow	34″ & wide
Drum material	Enamel	Enamel	Stainless steel	Enamel	Stainless steel
Loading	Top	Front	Front	Front	Front
Front porthole	Yes/No	Yes	Yes	Yes	Yes
Capacity	5 kilos	4 kilos	6 kilos	5 kilos	6 kilos
Spin speed	700 rpm	400 rpm	850 rpm	600 rpm	800 rpm
Water heating system	No[2]	Yes	Yes[3]	Yes	No[2]
Styling features	Inconspicuous appearance	Brightly colored	Indestructible appearance	Elegant appearance	Strong appearance
Washing action	Agitator	Tumble	Tumble	Agitator	Tumble

[1] 34″ height was in the process of being adopted as a standard work-surface height in Europe.
[2] "No," because most U.K. and Swedish homes had centrally heated hot water.
[3] "Yes," because Germans preferred to launder at temperatures higher than generally provided centrally.

The incremental variable unit costs of customizing to just a few of the preferences of each national market were as follows:

Stainless steel vs. enamel drum	£1.00
Porthole window	.10
Spin speed of 800 rpm vs. 700 rpm	.15
Water heater	2.15
6 vs. 5 kilos capacity	1.10

£6.10 = $18.20 at the
exchange rate of
that time.

The costs of customizing to the other preferences would have involved considerable plant investment, as well as additional variable costs. At the time the lowest retail prices (in pounds sterling) of leading locally produced brands in the various countries were:

U.K.	£110
France	£114
Germany	£113
Sweden	£134
Italy	£ 57

Unfortunately, product customization to the preferred specifications of each country would have put Hoover into poorly price-competitive positions in each of those countries, owing partly to these product extras but also substantially to the higher manufacturing costs incurred simply by having short production runs of machines with each separate feature. Since this was before the Common Market tariff-reduction programs became effective, Hoover also suffered from the additional competitive disadvantage of tariff duties in each Continental country.

Yet an imaginatively systematic analysis of actual automatic sales in each of these countries would have revealed the following incongruities:

1. Italian automatics, small in capacity and size, low-powered, without built-in heaters, with porcelain-enamel tubs, but aggressively low-priced, had substantial market shares in all countries, including Germany, and everywhere they were gaining share rapidly.
2. The by far best-selling automatics in Germany were ideally suited to the indicated German preferences but also were by far the highest-priced machines available in that country. They were also by far the most heavily advertised machines, by a factor of 3 to 1 over the next most-promoted brand.
3. Italy, with the lowest penetration of washing machines of any kind, was rapidly going directly to automatics, skipping over the pattern in other nations, where people went first to hand-wringer manually assisted machines and then to semi-automatic and finally to automatic machines. First-time Italian machine buyers generally bought the aggressively priced small fully automatics.
4. Cold-water and tepid-water laundering was just beginning to be promoted by detergent manufacturers, as had been successfully done in the United States by both detergent and machine manufacturers.

The growing success of small, low-powered, low-speed, low-capacity, low-priced Italian machines, even in Germany against the remarkable success of the preferred but most highly priced and most highly promoted German brand, contained a message that would not be noticed by people wedded confidently to a distorted version of the marketing concept—that you provide the customer with what is wanted rather than blindly with what you want to produce.

The message was clear enough for anyone with imagination and effort to see: In prevailing conditions people preferred, as in the case of the Italian equipment, the low-priced automatic over the manual or semi-automatic equipment, and certainly over higher-priced automatics, regardless of the failure of low-priced automatics to fulfill all their expressed preferences as to features. This was true even of the supposedly meticulous and uncompromising Germans, though the low-priced machines violated strong German preferences as to superheated water temperature, spinning speed, and size of equipment. And equally clear is that people were profoundly subject to promotional influence when it came to automatic washers, for in Germany, again, the most heavily promoted "ideal" machine was also by far the most highly priced and had the highest market share.

The combined message of these two facts is also clear enough: People wanted automatic rather than manual or semi-automatic home laundry equipment. There were two ways in which they were influenced to buy that preference—by low price, regardless of other preferred product features, and by heavy promotion, regardless of price. Both helped homemakers get what they most wanted, the superior benefits bestowed by fully automatic machines.

The message for Hoover should have been obvious: produce only the simple, high-quality machine preferred by the British and sell that same machine aggressively on the Continent at the powerfully competitive low price afforded by the 17 percent cost reduction that the elimination of £6.10 worth of extra features made possible. Suggested retail prices could have been somewhat under £100, with a sufficient extra pool of funds "saved" from the then unneeded plant modifications to support a service network and to launch aggressive media promotions on the Continent. The media message should have been that *this* is the machine that "you," the homemaker, *deserve* to have, and by means of which your relentlessly repetitive heavy daily household burdens are reduced, so that *you* may spend more constructive time for more elevating attention to your children and more loving attention to your husband. Indeed, communications should have targeted wife and husband jointly so as to implant in the latter, preferably in the presence of the former, a sense of obligation to provide an automatic washer for her even before an automobile for himself.

An aggressively low price, made possible by European standardization, combined with heavy promotion to the common global desire for alleviation from menial and repetitive work, and the common desire for enhanced familial and connu-

36

bial relations, would have overcome all previously expressed preferences as to special equipment features. Such a program would have reflected understanding of the "one great thing" about everybody: People everywhere want their burdens lightened, and they will pay to do so if they can afford it and are told how.

No matter how good the execution of a country-customized product strategy would have been, it would certainly have been suboptimal, and probably a failure. The issue was not execution but conception; not to do things right, but to do the right things.

The whole project got off on the wrong foot. It asked people what they wanted in the way of features alone rather than seeing what they visibly wanted as to life itself. The idea of a responsively responsible line of products tailored attentively to each nation not only would have been dumb but, even worse, would have been thoughtless. Unconscious of its dumbness and thoughtlessness, it would have asked, with erroneous pride in having practiced the marketing concept to its fullest, the wrong questions. In actual fact, it practiced that concept not at all. It merely looked at data and applied to them neither thought nor imagination—like the anthropocentrists in the Middle Ages who with everyday clarity saw the sun revolving in predictable ellipses around the earth, as opposed to Copernicus, who interpreted a more compelling reality, having no more data than they, but a more searching mind.

With much effort and imagination, Copernicus, like the hedgehog, knew everything about one great thing. The one great thing that distinguishes the global from the multinational corporation is that it accepts the reality of modernity, in which the republic of technology drives everything relentlessly toward global convergence, for better or for worse—toward the alleviation of life and the expansion of discretionary time and spending power. The new role of the global corporation is, in that respect, profoundly different from what has been the role of the ordinary corporation in its brief, turbulent, and remarkably protean history. The role of the global corporation is to orchestrate commercially the irresistible vectors of technology and globalization into benign benefactions for all the globe's inhabitants. It is a role created not by fate or nature or God, but by the necessity of open commerce itself, a necessity that compels action in which only the fit and the brave prosper and survive.

In the United States that necessity imposed itself on two of the nation's industries long before they became consciously aware of it. After more than a generation of regular and acrimonious industrywide labor shutdowns, there has not been an industrywide strike by the United Steelworkers union since 1959 or by the United Automobile Workers union of General Motors (which would shut down two-thirds of U.S. production), since 1970. Both reflect the realization that these industries had become global, that shutting down U.S. manufacturing would not shut out U.S. customers. Overseas suppliers helped keep customers in operation and reduced domestic competitive viability. Globalization of competition compelled domestic adjustment to realities to which the unions accommodated before the companies themselves.

Since the emergence of the marketing concept a quarter of a century ago, the more managerially advanced corporations of the Western world have been driven by a responsive eagerness to produce for customers what they clearly wanted rather than merely trying to sell them what was being produced. This has been accompanied by the creation of awesomely large and costly marketing departments complete with ponderously professional market researchers. It has also resulted in extraordinary product-line and operations proliferations—highly tailored products and delivery systems for many different markets, market segments, and nations.

We have witnessed also, more recently, the extraordinary success of Japanese companies all around the globe. Significantly, they operate almost entirely without marketing departments or market research of the kind so prevalent in the West. Yet, in the colorful words of John F. Welch, Jr., General Electric's chief executive, the Japanese, coming from a small chain of resource-poor islands on the other side of the globe, from an entirely alien culture, with an almost impenetrably complex language, have "cracked the code" of western markets. They have done it not by looking with mechanistic thoroughness at how markets and customers are different, but rather like Copernicus, by searching for meaning with a deeper wisdom. This has led them to discover the one great thing all relevant markets have in common. That is the overwhelming desire for dependable, world-standard modernity in all things, and at aggressively low prices, even "low" in the higher-priced product categories and customer segments.

The lower the price the greater the likelihood that the world will accept standardized modernity in all its major sectors and segments rather than insist on higher-priced customization to inherited preferences and ancient practices. The more world standardization and lower prices expand world markets, the lower the production and delivery costs with which to push prices down and expand markets further. This is an old truth clearly recognized during the early stages of the Industrial Revolution, when the British textile industry dominated world markets even in their most inaccessible and primitive backwaters. And today the Japanese typically deliver value that is irresistible everywhere, even to people and places that market-research technocrats conclude with superficial certainty have proliferated varities of product and delivery preferences that push costs and prices ever upward and increasingly out of customer and competitive reach.

To speak of global convergence and commonality is not to ignore the persistence of important differences between nations, areas, and cultures. But this requires making some distinctions. The difference between a distinction and a difference is that differences are perfectly consistent with fundamental underlying and surrounding samenesses. Persistent differences can complement rather than simply oppose the advancement of commonalities—in society and business no less than in physics and space. There is, simultaneously, matter and antimatter. The earth is round, but for most purposes in everyday life it's sensible to treat it as flat. Space is curved, but not much for most purposes here on earth.

The Chinese are different in a whole variety of visible ways from the Germans and the Zimbabwe, but still all three are remarkably alike regarding love, hate, fear, greed, envy, joy, patriotism, pornography, material comforts, mysticism, and the role of food in their lives. The world is driven and held together by the common bonds that unite its differences. Increasingly, modern times create new bonds of commonality that, in themselves, cause lots of problems and raise lots of questions. But how problematical are those problems, how quizzical those questions? Consider Maine and California. It takes no special talents to see the differences—the differences between the socially avant-garde and the socially rear guard; between L. L. Bean and Frederick's of Hollywood; between Silicon Valley and the Penobscot Valley; between Bar Harbor and Muscle Beach or the Mendocino coast.

Yet with all these persistent differences, consider the persuasive evidence of the homogenizing character of American life. If a large nation can be so thoroughly homogenized by the combinative forces of tradition, technology, aspirations, and communications, and yet retain powerfully persistent and significant differences within its borders, then it's reasonable to suggest that commonality can also advance and thrive among disparate nations and regions.

The wider a company's global reach, then the larger the number of differences it is likely to encounter as to national and regional preferences regarding product features, distribution institutions, promotional media, and the like.

Nor is there any presumption, as we have seen, that differences in preferences as to product features, tastes, and market arrangements are largely confined to high-touch products. Evolution does not move linearly along perfectly parallel lines in all parts of the world's disparateness, even in this world of microprocessor modernity. In the United States almost all manufacturers of microprocessors check them for reliability and functionality by what's called the parallel testing system. In Japan, the preference is almost totally for the much different sequential testing system. The result is that Teradyne Corp., the world's largest producer of microprocessor test equipment, makes one line for the United States and one for Japan. That's easy. What's not so easy, and is equally problematic for other firms facing similar situations, is how to organize and manage the marketing effort. The possibilities are to organize by product, by region, by function, or by some matrix combination. Thus, one might have separate marketing organizations for Japan and for the United States, the former obviously specializing in parallel test equipment and the latter in sequential test equipment. Or one might organize by product, the one group ending up working largely in Japan and the other in the United States. A single manufacturing facility might produce both systems, with a single marketing operation that sells both, or a separate marketing operation for each, and the like. If the system is organized by product, should the group that handles the parallel system, whose major market is in the United States, also attempt a sales effort in Japan, thus competing with the sequential group that is focused solely on the Japan market? And vice versa? If the effort is organized regionally, how do the regional groups divide their efforts between pushing (should they?) the parallel system and pushing the sequential system? If the company is organized by function, how do you get commitment in marketing, for example, for one line as against the other?

The point is obvious enough. A major problem in a world of increasing global commonality is how to organize and manage in the face of persistent differences in the context of a generalized drift toward and preference for standardization.

There is no formula to answer that question, not even a satisfactory contingent one. What may work well for one company in a given situation may fail for another in that very same situation. The reasons have to do with the capabilities, the histories, the reputations, the resources, and even the cultures and spirits of the two organizations. In that respect the governing determinants of success are no different from those of success in love and courtship. Even limited experience in such matters affirms that under identical conditions different people will perform differently, that what works for one person in that situation may not for another. The contingencies that prescribe what's important do not predictably define what's appropriate. Not even specific knowledge of the specific actors is enough to assure the appropriateness of the advice. As one would not, in affairs of love, give in a specific situation the same advice to Marcello Mastroianni as to Woody Allen, so also one would not in affairs of commerce give the same advice in a specific situation to Olivetti and IBM, or to Banco di Roma and Credit Lyonnais.[3]

Differences persist. The distinction between the past and the future is that technology and economics favor commonality, forcing onto the modern corporation, regardless of size, the necessity constantly to reach out for adaptation to what's new while functioning effectively with what remains unchanged and abides.

One of the most powerful yet also least celebrated ways in which commerce is being driven toward global standardization is via the monetary system and the international investment process.

In today's times money is simply electronic impulses. With the speed of light it gets moved effortlessly between distant money centers (and even lesser places). A change of ten basis points in the price of a bond will cause an instant and massive shift of money from, say, London to Tokyo. This has profound effects on how companies throughout the world operate. Even Japan, with its high debt-to-equity balance sheets that are "guaranteed" to the banks by various presumptions in that society regarding the superior virtue of "the long view," or "guaranteed" in other ways by government policy—even there, upward shifts in interest rates in other parts of the world attract capital in proportions that are powerfully felt. This accounts for the rising proportion in recent years of Japanese global corporations going to the world's equity markets for funds. Debt is simply too remunerative in other high-yielding countries to keep enough at home to feed the Japanese need for capital. And as

[3] For some recent evidence of the contingent nature of all this, see Christopher Bartlett, "MNCs: Get off the reorganization merry-go-round," *Harvard Business Review,* March/April 1983; and C. Bartlett, Y. Doz, and C. K. Prahalad, "Global Competitive Pressures and Host Country Demands: Managing Tensions in MNC's," *California Management Review,* Spring 1981.

interest rates rise, equity becomes for the issuer a more attractive option. The effect on Japanese enterprise will be increasingly transforming. As the equity proportions of Japanese companies' capitalizations rise, so will their need to respond to the shorter-term investment horizons of the equity markets. Thus the much-vaunted Japanese corporate advantage of being able, because of their capital structures, to take "the long view" rather than requiring early results will gradually disappear. Driven thus increasingly to respond to the equity market's demand for early results, so the world will also increasingly be driven toward a common convergence in the forces that influence how business is conducted, not just in how business responds to its markets.

On all fronts, globalization converges into a common coalescence. The differences that persist affirm a fixed and ancient dictum of economics—namely, that the world is driven by what happens at the margin or at the appendages, not at the core; that significance attaches not to the common or typical or average condition but rather to the edges of events. Thus, in ordinary competitive analysis, economics affirms that what's important is not the average price but the marginal price, the price at the unstable interface of newly erupting conditions. What counts in commercial affairs is not what's predominantly happening but what's happening at the cutting edge; not the persistent and predominant differences among nations regarding tastes, preferences, and practices, but the underlying similarity of what happens increasingly to them all at the margin, forces that cumulate everywhere into an overwhelming and predominant commonality.

Nor is it useful to refer in contrast to the persistence of a vast variety of trade and tax barriers that block the globalization of markets. Economic nationalism and various philistine reinforcers are not likely to disappear. They have a powerful persistence. But, as in the case of the globalization of investment funds, the world gets shaped by more than the past alone. It does not remain a fixed paradigm, dominated unyieldingly by immemorial custom and derived attitudes, regardless of the intervening forces of technology and realism. Cosmopolitanism is no longer the monopoly of the intellectual and leisure classes. It has become the established property and defining characteristic of business society itself. Gradually and irresistibly it breaks down the walls of economic insularity, nationalism, and chauvinism. What we see today as escalating commercial nationalism is simply the last violent death rattle of an obsolete institution.

The successful global corporation does not abjure customization or differentiation for the requirements of markets that differ in product preferences, spending patterns, shopping preferences, and institutional and legal arrangements. But the global corporation accepts and adjusts to these differences only reluctantly, only after relentlessly testing their immutability—after trying in various ways to circumvent and reshape them, as we shall see with some examples shortly.

Different market segments and institutional arrangements will always remain the world over, as they do within single countries. That's not the point. The point is that there is increasing and rapid global convergence in all the big things that drive commerce and industry. The world's inherited old varieties of distinctive national economic institutions and practices, its inherited old varieties of distinctive national preferences as to product characteristics and features, and all its other inherited old varieties of culture-bound national attributes that have historically required the almost total domestication of international corporate activities to the requirements of each separate nation —all these rest now on increasingly shaky ground. The world is becoming increasingly informed about the liberating and enhancing possibilities of modernity. The persistence of the past rests uneasily on increased evidence of, and restlessness regarding, its inefficiency, costliness, and confinements. The historical past and the national differences respecting commerce and industry it spawned and fostered everywhere are now subject to relatively easy transformation. It will take only imagination, effort, and persistence by those who accept the truth about the one great thing that dominates life everywhere and who therefore set out with standardized products and practices, and with aggressive prices, to create world-scale markets eager for modernity. In this regard, Henry Kissinger observes, in his book

Years of Upheaval, of the continued Japanese economic successes the world over, "What could be more effective than a society voracious in its collection of information, impervious to pressure and implacable in execution?"

There is an opposing argument about how technology can now drive the world. My argument for the growing globalization of markets clearly rests on two premises regarding customer behavior: (1) the homogenization of the world's wants, and (2) people's willingness to sacrifice specific preferences in product features, functions, design, and the like for lower prices at high quality. Lower prices, I have argued, are facilitated by the scale economies of production, transportation, and communication that massive global markets will make possible.

The counter argument is not trivial. It says that the rapidly growing development of flexible factory automation will enable plants of massive size to change products and product features quickly, even without actually stopping the manufacturing process, so that they can produce broad lines of almost customized products without sacrificing the scale economies that come from long production runs of standardized items. Indeed, computer-aided design and manufacturing (CAD/CAM), combined with robotics, will create a new equipment and process technology (EPT) that will make small plants located close to their markets as efficient as larger ones located distantly, hastening ever faster the competitive superiority of Professor C. Wickham Skinner's famous "focused factory." It will not be economies of scale that will dominate, but rather economies of scope—the ability of either large or small plants to produce great varieties of relatively customized products at remarkably low costs. And if that happens, the counter argument says, customers will have no need to abandon in the market place their special preferences. These preferences can be satisfied at the same low prices as standardized products—perhaps at even lower prices, because the new flexible factories are newer and more efficient simply because they are new, not only because they are different.

I will not deny the power of these possibilities, or even the suggestion that the economics of the Industrial Revolution will be replaced by the new economics of the digital revolution. But possibilities do not probabilities make. There is no conceivable way in which flexible factory automation dedicated to producing many customized lines of a specific product can achieve the scale economies of an equally modernized plant dedicated to the massive production of narrow standardized lines of that product. The new digitized equipment and process technologies are available to all. This will enable those with minimal customization and narrow product-line breadth to drive their costs, as in old-fashioned mass production, far below those with more customization and wider lines.

Combining this fact with the global homogenization of taste and preferences that is in such obvious ascent, and with everything we know about the one great thing we all have in common everywhere—namely, the necessity of our insatiable wants to accommodate to our limited financial capabilities—it follows that people will prefer in overwhelming numbers lower-priced, more-or-less standardized quality products over higher-priced customized products. That has been true throughout the recorded history of humankind. It is not reasonable to suppose that the microprocessor, for all its fabulous fungibility, will change what's so powerfully built into our immemorial genes.

It will be said that even though the world moves relentlessly toward product commonality, this does not hold true for the institutions through which products flow. There is a strong prevailing belief in the immutability of distribution channels, for example, and their accompanying institutions that vary so widely in kind, structure, and stages of development around the world. It is known, of course, that things can and do change over time. But the belief in immutability remains strongly entrenched, modified only to the extent of belief also in evolution and gradualism.

What is seldom even imagined are the possibilities of vigorous and yet patient intervention to modify, transform, or bypass established channels and practices. There is abundant evidence that this is both possible and effective. Not that there have not been horrendous setbacks or failures. In Japan, Revlon unnecessarily alienated retailers and confused customers by first selling world-standardized products only in elite outlets and then tried rapidly to recover with low-price world-standardized products in broader distribution, again rapidly followed by changing the Japanese company president and making distribution cutbacks as costs rose faster than sales. The problem was not, as some have argued, that Revlon didn't understand the Japanese market. The problem was irresolution and impatience. By contrast, in Europe the Outboard Marine Corporation, by imagination, push, and persistence, not only collapsed long-established three-step distribution channels (primary, secondary, dealer) to a more controlled and focussed two-step system, and against the overwhelmingly knowledgeable and foreboding advice of local trade groups, but also vastly reduced the number and types of its retail outlets. The result was major improvement in credit and product-installation service to retail customers, major cost reductions, and major sales advances.

In its highly successful Japanese introduction of Contac 600 (the time-release anticongestant), SmithKline Corporation distributed to all forty-seven prefectures via only thirty-five wholesalers instead of the thousand or more somewhat unruly ones that established practice was presumed to require. This was accompanied by certain special daily contacts with the wholesalers and key retailers, also in violation of established practice, but it worked.

Similarly, Komatsu, the Japanese manufacturer of world-standardized lightweight farm machinery, being denied access to established distribution institutions in the United States, successfully entered the market by selling through over-the-road construction equipment dealers in rural areas of the Sun Belt. It went to a part of the United States where farms were smaller and equipment needs less muscular, letting product appropriateness and price attract customers to uncommon distributors. In a vast variety of electronic office equipment and retail checkout registers, the Japanese sold, at the outset in the United States, not through conventional channels using established methods but through electrical repair shops with no previous experience in either the equipment or in sales.

In all these cases supposedly immutable institutional arrangements were circumvented, shattered, or transformed by the combination of product modernity and reliability, strong and sustained support systems, aggressive low prices, aggressive sales-compensation packages, and often these generally combined with audacity and implacability. Instead of producing resentment or disreputability in the entered markets, they produced admiration and awe.

Divergences of these kinds from established practice actually happen all the time everywhere, but they seem natural when done by home-country companies at home. The multinational mind, warped into circumspection and timidity by years of horrific stumbles and stories about transnational troubles, now rarely contemplates departure from presumptively fixed practices in other lands. Indeed, too often it considers even the thought of such departure as mindless, disrespectful, impossible. It is the mind of a bygone day.

In only one significant respect are a company's activities around the world important, and that is what and how it produces and sells. Everything else is derivative from, and subsidiary to, these activities. What is produced and how it is sold represent what is uniquely the corporate purpose.

The purpose of business is to get and keep a customer. Or, to use Peter Drucker's more demanding construction, to *create* and keep a customer. The business does this by being wedded constructively to the ideal of innovation, seeking constantly to offer better or more preferred products in such combinations of ways, means, places, and at such prices as to make prospects *prefer* in some acceptable proportion to do business with itself rather than with others. Preferences are constantly being shaped and reshaped. The significance of modern times resides in how technology is shaping the world's preferences into homogenized commonality—into global standardization. Within that commonality enormous variety constantly asserts itself and thrives, as can be seen within the world's single largest domestic market, the United States. But in the process of the world's being shaped into the kind of homogenizing commonality I have been talking about something else clearly happens, namely, the expansion of modern markets into cost-reducing global proportions.

Thus, two vectors operate simultaneously to drive the world: the vector of technology and the vector of globalization. The first helps powerfully to shape human preferences. The second shapes economic realities. With preferences converging, regardless of how much they constantly evolve and also diverge, markets are shaped into magnitudes that allow great economies of scale and therefore reduction of costs and prices.

The modern global corporation, as contrasted to the aging multinational corporation, "impervious to pressure and implacable in execution," seeks constantly to hasten the consummation of what already occurs, to force suitably standardized products and practices onto the entire globe, because that is, indeed, exactly what the world will take, especially when aggressively low prices are linked to quality and reliability.

Given what is everywhere the purpose of a business, the global business, in the spirit of the hedgehog, will shape the vectors of technology and globalization into a great, single strategic fecundity for itself. It will systematically push these vectors toward a converging center, where optimization of high-quality global standardization produces optimally low costs, optimally low prices, and therefore, in combination, optimal patronage at optimal profits for itself. Reciprocally, this means companies that do not adapt to the new global realities will become the victims of those that do and prosper.

3

The Industrialization of
Service

The service sector of industrially advanced nations has
been in proportional ascent for nearly three-quarters of a century. In the United States in the past twenty years alone, the
non-goods-producing sector of the nonagricultural labor force
rose 40 percent faster than the goods-producing sector.

It would be redundant to recite once more the growing
share of the nation's GNP that the so-called service sector occupies. Nor is it just the expanding proportions taken up by the
multiplicity of government, school district, and other public em-
ployments that have produced this increase, though civilian public employment alone rose nearly four times faster in the past
twenty years than goods-producing employment.

Actually, there is a massive hidden service sector: that proportion of nominally "manufacturing" industries whose ex-

penses and revenues largely represent pre- and postpurchase servicing in the form of systems planning, preinstallation support, "software," repair, maintenance, delivery, collection, bookkeeping, and the like.

As the industrialization in the rest of the world gradually catches up with the more advanced nations, some say, the advanced nations will lose their relative advantage. The shift in the developing nations from craft to industrial labor, from hand work to machine work, produces great vaulting increases in productivity. Meanwhile, in the already industrialized nations affluence and discretionary spending shift demand increasingly into low-productivity, labor-intensive service activities—automotive repair, travel, commercial lodging, entertainment, restaurants, shopping, insurance brokerage, medical care, education, and the like. The result, so the argument goes, is that the advanced nations lose their advantage even faster than the developing nations expand their manufacturing industries.

In the advanced industrial nations this has of late produced a paradoxical paranoia—the proposition that their expanding service appetites shift consumer and industrial demand in directions that are little susceptible to the employment of mass-production efficiencies, which, in time, leads to rising general price levels and finally to retarded (even reduced) living standards. Since it costs more to buy the less efficiently produced services, one's money doesn't go as far. Moreover, for the nation intent on maintaining some sort of world trade competitiveness, it will have to tighten its belt, which reduces living standards even more.

Those are the supposed cybernetics of world economics: Advantage leads ultimately to a demand for costly service amenities while producing a parallel no-frills catch-up effort among the less advantaged, who finally not only catch up but surpass the original leaders because, for one thing, their technology is more modern.

Japan, Germany, and Hong Kong are dramatic examples of no-frills catch-up. Britain is a dismal example of having been caught up on and now left pathetically behind.

THE END IS NOT IN SIGHT

But Britain is also a particularly apt example for showing that the fears of accelerating disadvantage in the developed world and of retarded living standards in the more advanced service-intensive industrial nations are not necessarily justified. Britain shows, particularly by comparison with the United States, that the rising proportion of GNP devoted to so-called service activities need not necessarily produce a parallel and equivalent decline in either absolute or relative national productivity.

In the United States the service sector has demonstrated a remarkable capacity to improve productivity, while in Britain it has exhibited the polar opposite, an almost obsessive persistence of ancient service practices that drain the economy of competitive vitality. In Britain, "to serve" remains to this day encrusted with immemorial attachments to master–servant pretensions that dull the imagination and block the path to service efficiency. In spite of spectacularly rising British retail prices, laws have been passed to resist the construction and growth of that new marvel of retailing efficiency, the hypermarché (the superstore). More efficient even than the American supermarket and the general-merchandise mass marketer, the hypermarché has been effectively resisted by coalitions of small personal-service retailers and local and national politicians.

This British resistance to retailing efficiency reflects the traditional insularity of the petty bourgeoisie. It is, in fact, a profoundly persistent cultural manifestation with ancestral roots in distant centuries. Historically there have always been class distinctions, and not just in Britain. The lower classes have always been obliged to serve and fawn for the benefit of those above them. "Service" took the form of one person's labor for the benefit of another—the butler, the footman, the parlor maid, the upstairs maid, the solicitor, the butcher, the greengrocer, the tailor, and the cook, all performing one-on-one, highly personalized service, whether laying out the clothes or cutting the roast just right to the exacting specifications of each familiar customer in the shop. To this day, with Britain teetering precariously on the economic edge, even moderately priced restaurants are redundantly populated with paid factotums in frayed sartorial imitations of the past, each specializing in a separate and costly triviality, like opening doors, removing and carrying coats to the cloakroom (there manned by yet another), removing dirty ashtrays from tables but not dirty dishes. And in offices, the prodigality of worn-out and outworn retainers ever present to run errands and perform menial personal services is visible everywhere, doing questionably required work that incurs unquestionably real expenses and serves no real purpose. The purpose served is purely ceremonial: keeping up, with senile thoughtlessness, with appearances that have no merit save that of decayed grace and mannered tawdriness. Things add up, not only in their measurable pecuniary costs, but also in the way people think about the work to be done and how to do it.

As I shall elaborate more fully in Chapter 9, as long as we cling to preindustrial notions about what service is and does—the idea that to serve means to humble oneself before another, to toady and to acquiesce, to respond to orders and custom rather than think about the function to be performed with the new tools that are available and the new systems that are possible—as long as we think of service as being next to servility; of "serving" as a synonym for thoughtless obedience; of service as a lower occupation (when it comes to work) or a higher occupation (when it comes to the elite professions, like the clergy and the military, where the premium is on ecclesiastical faith and marshal obedience, not on thought or independence), as long as these sterile notions of a vanished world dominate our own thoughts and attitudes, none of the applied rationality that has produced such magnificently thrusting efficiencies in the industrial system will be brought to bear on what remains today an unconscionably retarded maze of inefficiencies in the service sectors that surround that system.

The foregoing examples of service wastefulness still present in modern Britain illustrate a general rule about endurance: Things may be obsolescent though not obsolete. All this may be less so in the United States, but in the case of the ancient fetters that enthrall our attitudes toward and shape the quality of our service work, everywhere their endurance carries a common presumption that service literally means, and will be best, when one person directly and personally attends another, much as a servant attends the master. As long as this presumption reigns, service will forever be limited in efficiency, reliability, and quality.

Opportunities for service improvement lie all around, and yet in the United States, where much improvement has already occurred, it has gone vastly unnoticed. We celebrate the glamorous work of heroic astronauts in distant places, accomplishing through science and technology deeds of speculative merit. But we ignore the practical accomplishments of people who daily all around us produce with lesser tools, simpler methods, and less elaborate organization, a constant stream of productive service results of more mundane but immediate merit. We shall see in the following pages exactly how amply we are benefited daily by so much we daily see but don't apprehend—and how these benefactions are the result of what I have called "the industrialization of service."

There is little reason why an industrialized but increasingly service-intensive economy should advance less rapidly than newly industrializing economies, though one may concede that technologically advanced economies may have some disadvantage regarding the rate of future productivity improvement. But I hope to show by concrete example that service activities are so enormously lagging behind existing potentials for improving their efficiency and productivity that a case can actually be made that advanced industrial nations can improve their overall productivity even more rapidly than the lagging developing nations that are so aggressively adopting modern industrial machinery and systems.

THE NEW SERVICE FECUNDITY

Go back to the hypermarché. Its forerunners in the United States are supermarkets and mass-merchandising discount stores. They are self-service stores, and that helps explain their

superior efficiency. Instead of a clerk behind the counter responding to each customer's special requests for items that must
then be individually fetched, weighed, and bagged, the customer
now does most of the work himself, and lots faster. The corner
grocery store in which the clerk was, like Benvenuto Cellini, a
careful craftsman personally putting the whole grocery list together and doing all the work associated with the customer's trip
to the store has been largely replaced by the supermarket assembly line. The customer alone assembles the purchase, moving
through the aisles and filling a cart from the store inventory
much as an automobile frame moves along a line and gets assembled from the plant inventory.

The supermarket and the mass-market discount store represent the industrialization of ancient craftsmanship. In both
cases there are tremendous economies, great efficiencies, and, I
would insist, a much better product. The modern automobile *is*
better—more uniformly reliable, cheaper, more durable and yet
still highly customized to the special specifications of millions of
individual buyers throughout the land, each with his own private
preferences that are rather satisfactorily served at remarkably
low costs. The independent craftsman might have constructed a
more uniquely personalized and interesting car, but also probably a more idiosyncratic one, embellishing the whole project
with elaborate little pirouettes expressing his own personal
style, perhaps quaintly ornamented or disastrously experimental. And so with the butcher at the older store. He might have
cut the roast more lovingly (or, as the case may be, more
shrewdly) and perhaps augmented it with the self-serving weight
of his own thumb on the scale—a more personal production,
certainly, but also less predictably reliable and certainly more
painfully costly.

The supermarket represents the industrialization of service.
It combines more space and capital in larger but fewer aggre-
gates. Gone, for the most part, are the ancient modes of ''service'' it displaced with new efficiencies, lower costs, and greater
customer satisfaction, altogether an efficient act of creative destruction.

There are numerous other ways in which service has already been industrialized. Most of us regularly see them at work; few of us are aware of them. Even fewer fully appreciate their revolutionizing importance for our lives and businesses. Only he without fresh air to breathe and food to eat fully appreciates their importance. It is worth a long look at the industrializing modes that already help make service more abundantly productive than it has been in the past. It will help focus effort and energize activity toward the use of these principles in other service activities.

Service can be industrialized in three ways: via hard technologies, soft technologies, and hybrid technologies.

The hard technologies are the most obvious. They substitute machinery, tools, or other tangible artifacts for people in the performance of service work. Thus:

1. The electrocardiogram reliably substitutes a lower-paid technician for the high-paid doctor listening unsteadily and unreliably with a stethoscope.
2. The consumer credit card and CRT credit and bank-balance checking machine replace a long and embarrassing manual credit check for each purpose.
3. Airport X-ray surveillance equipment replaces a long, messy, and embarrassing manual rummaging through baggage.
4. The automatic car wash replaces the uneven quality and personality-destroying work of individuals washing by hand.
5. The Polaroid Land Camera replaces film that must be returned and processed in an essentially people-intensive plant.
6. Automatic toll collectors at bridges, subway entrances, and elsewhere replace human collectors.
7. The home is full of hard technologies replacing people: automatic washers, precooked convenience foods, never-needs-ironing clothing, and chemically treated dirt-resistant clothing, floor covering, and upholstered furniture.

Soft technologies are essentially the substitution of organized preplanned systems for individual service operatives.

Often these involve some modification of the tools (or technologies) employed, but their essential feature is the system itself, where special hardware or routies are specifically designed to produce the desired results:

1. Supermarkets and other self-service establishments like cafeterias, restaurant salad bars, open tool rooms in factories, open-stack libraries.

2. Fast-food restaurants: McDonald's, Burger Chef, Pizza Hut, Dunkin' Donuts, Kentucky Fried Chicken, and the like. I have elsewhere explained these in detail. There I pointed out the intricate planning these systems require, the division of labor that's entailed—some workers prepare only the meat for the hamburger in a central commissary, some only the buns, some the salads, and so forth. At point of sale the same rational system of specialization is rigorously followed to produce speed, quality control, cleanliness, cheerfulness, and low prices.

3. Prepackaged vacation tours that obviate the need for extensive and time-consuming personal selling, extensive tailoring of the product to numerous different kinds of customers, and a great deal of price haggling. American Express probably has the largest variety of packages, handsomely presented, described, and promoted in a brochure of magazine proportions. Significantly this, too, is like an assembly line in principle. American Express seldom creates or operates the tours. That's done mostly by others. American Express mostly assembles and packages the information and sells the product for those who deliver it.

4. Off-the-shelf insurance programs, packaged and unalterable, except via the selection of other packages. Allstate Insurance was the mass-market pioneer, though preceded by the old "industrial" insurance salesman who sold door-to-door and collected weekly, and more recently imitated by off-the-shelf insurance-by-mail.

5. Mutual funds, as against one-at-a-time stock selection, the latter filled with ambiguities, uncertainties, and repetitive reselling and reeducation with each transaction.

57

6. Christmas Club and payroll-deduction savings systems, both one-time selling and one-time deciding situations, and thereafter automatically and routinely and cheaply executed.
7. Bank-by-mail systems.
8. Carefully planned routing systems for salesmen to reduce travel time and maximize sales and service time.
9. Fully systematized, production-line, yet personalized income tax preparation service on a walk-in basis, performed at remarkably low cost with remarkable accuracy and guarantees. The pioneer and master merchant is, of course, H. & R. Block.

Finally, there are the hybrid technologies. They combine hard equipment with carefully planned industrial systems to bring efficiency, order, and speed to the service process:

1. Computer-based over-the-road truck utilization and routing. By careful programming for types and grades of roads, location of stops, congestion of roads, toll-road costs, and mixing-point access, it optimizes truck utilization and minimizes user cost. Its most extensive and complex incarnation is Cummins Engine's "Power Management Program."
2. Radio-controlled ready-mix concrete truck routing, rerouting, and delivery, pioneered early and to an advanced state by Texas Industries of Dallas.
3. Development of unit trains and integral trains that carry, over great distances, a single commodity (coal by the Baltimore & Ohio Railroad and grain by the Illinois Central are common examples) with few or no intermediate stops, thus providing fast long runs at such enormous efficiency that they can deadhead back and still save money. The system requires enormous logistical synchronization at point of origin, at destination, and in between. Its value? In the case of the B&O, its original unit train reduced the round-trip time between West Virginia's coal fields and Baltimore from twenty-one days to seven.

4. Preorder shipment of perishables at long distances, for example, sending trainloads of lemons in California (pioneered by Sunkist) east before orders have been placed, using weather forecasting services for intermediate routing and dropoffs in time to reach cities where expected high temperatures will raise the consumption of lemonade and Tom Collinses. Any lost hot day is a lost day of sales. Weyerhauser pioneered a similar system for shipping lumber east, in this case to provide it with an inventory-free "instant" delivery capability to distant customers.

5. Limited-service, fast, low-priced repair facilities, such as national muffler and transmission shops, originally pioneered by Midas. High volume, specialization, and special-purpose tools combine to produce fast, guaranteed results.

6. In order to assess the degree of risk and determine the terms of a proposed financing service with its potential clients, a major financial services company routinely sent teams of auditors to its prospects to evaluate each individual account in their accounts receivable ledgers. The field auditors made and checked all entries by hand. When these auditors were equipped with portable computing systems, the result was an 80 percent reduction in the number of man-hours required for field transactions, including the generation of immediate bids for the jobs on the clients' sites.

These are fairly familiar, though seldom acknowledged, examples of the substitution of hard, soft, and hybrid technologies (that is, of machines and of organized systems of work, or combinations thereof) for ancient, preindustrial modes of work that was always done as an extension of the craft culture, either one-on-one by servant for master or in a primitive industrial fashion that merely substituted a more powerful or efficient machine (say, the locomotive or the steam shovel) for a weaker or less capacitous predecessor (say, the horse or the spade.) Fortunately, there is a huge array of additional possibilities, some of them not nearly so obvious as to potential, and many considerably more promising than even their visible potential at first suggests. The failure of so many of us to recognize that these opportunities exist, or even to appreciate where applications have already been made or to appreciate that these represent a profound divergence from and improvement upon preindustrial concepts of service—that failure is a measure of how firmly we remain tethered by the confining fetters of an ancient heritage. Even when we invent profoundly significant new things, we remain unaware of what we have achieved and therefore unalerted to the possibilities of the application of those same disciplines to what yet remains to be done.

THE SPECIAL CASES OF SPECIAL OPPORTUNITIES

"You just can't get reliable repair service any more"—so goes the national refrain. It is such a persistent refrain that we are immediately justified in automatically doubting its veracity. When the General Electric Service Corporation's clean white radio-dispatched repair truck pulls into my driveway, I *know* I'm going to get better and more reliable TV service than in the bad old days of the underinventoried, questionably trained, variably priced (what the market would bear, usually), soiled serviceman in his used pickup truck. I am considerably more confident at the Exxon Repair Center with twelve fully equipped, fully lighted, temperature-controlled work stations, with uniformed certified mechanics, where prices are posted, estimates made clearly in advance, and where the completed work is ready as promised when I return at five o'clock.

Yet it is precisely these kinds of service activities that have room for the most improvement. They require as a precondition to high efficiency and low cost precisely the same sorts of disciplines and strategies that make modern manufacturing so efficient and low-cost. They require (1) the application of industrial modes of thinking to the organization of the service effort and (2), often, large amounts of capital.

60

For the Exxon Repair Center to be efficient it requires, first, division of labor. A trained transmission expert worth $10 an hour must not work at such minimum-wage jobs as changing transmission oil. Nor would one let a minimum-wage transmission-oil-changer try to repair the transmission. In order to enjoy the advantages of division of labor, one needs a lot of volume. That requires a large plant occupying lots of land; fully equipped with costly new labor-saving tools and diagnostic and repair machinery; professionally managed; and promoted and advertised with sufficient frequency and persuasability to draw large numbers of motorists from a wide area. This would, in turn, probably require pickup and delivery services to make up for the inconvenience of motorists having to come long distances. All this is costly. Thus, efficiency in service can require as much investment in plant, equipment, and promotion as has been historically associated with efficiency in manufacturing. It can require as much planning, organization, training, controls, and capital as produced the original car at the outset. It requires, in short, a different way of thinking about what service is, what it can be made to be, and how it must be financed.

The key point is "volume"—magnitudes sufficient to achieve efficiency, sufficient to employ systems and technologies that produce reliable, rapid, and low-unit-cost results. And that, in turn, requires the kind of managerial rationality seldom seen or, indeed, needed in a small shop.

This same principle of magnitudes applies in other highly promising areas where its employment is now in its infancy.

1. Specialized, highly automated medical diagnostic clinics. The Damon Corporation operates 125 such clinics throughout the nation, which with the help of modern machines, 125 salaried M.D.'s, 22 Ph.D's, and 1,400 medical technologists perform a wide range of diagnostic tests that formerly required patients to visit several doctors and clinics at costs in time and money several multiples above Damon's.
2. Prepaid health service centers, comprising a wide range of specialists who can be kept fully employed at their

specialties. Pioneered by the Kaiser Foundation in Oakland, California, there are several hundred HMOs (Health Maintenance Organizations) all over the country whose members prepay annual "dues" for easy access to medical specialists and technicians working in central clinics equipped with the latest technologies and employed full time, without intervening administrative burdens, at their respective specialties, and only their specialties. Nor is low-cost, rapid, convenient health care confined to outpatient services. Since the formation of the first one in Phoenix, Arizona, in 1970 there are now more than a hundred ASFs (Ambulatory Surgical Facilities) in the United States. They typically are equipped to do some 125 low-risk operations on the healthy, low-risk patient. The typical facility has two or more operating rooms, a recovery area, and a diagnostic center. The patient comes in—say, for a tonsillectomy —undergoes tests and surgery, rests, and goes home, all in one day. At Northwest Surgicare, a for-profit ASF in the Chicago area, the total tonsillectomy bill a few years ago was $169, as against $548 at Chicago's nonprofit Michael Reese Hospital. The Metropolitan Insurance Company, which honored twenty-two ASFs under group insurance policies, estimates it had saved $1 million in three years.

3. Word processing stations, the system of centralized typing for offices, including the use of computerized self-correcting typewriters. Instead of numerous erratically busy secretaries scattered throughout a large company's offices or secretaries engaged in typing where their value is greater for other purposes, a great deal of routine typing is centralized into fully busy word processing centers where the fastest equipment becomes justified and scheduling and supervision become sensible.

4. Centralized food preparation commissaries that provide fresh and tasty delicatessen foods and sandwiches to large numbers at small convenience stores, private clubs, offices, and the like. In some cases (Steward's

Sandwiches Co., for example) these commissaries have route delivery systems and provide infrared and microwave ovens to their customers.

The second "special opportunity" category of service improvement resides in the design of products that often require postpurchase servicing. We shall call this the product/repair interface. Perhaps the best-known "solution" to the repair service problem is Motorola's (now Quasar's) highly advertised "works in a box" television design. Instead of emphasizing improved repair capability via improved repairman training (the ancient idea that to get better service requires getting better or better training of servicemen), Motorola simply eliminated the serviceman, or nearly so. Designed as a modular assembly, the television set is capable of "instant" repair by simply removing and replacing a major module that contains a defective part. A direct imitation of the military's concept of "third echelon maintenance," it emphasizes *fast restoration* rather than reliable repair. The military was clear enough about its needs: fast and reliable return to urgent duty at the front. So was Motorola: Get it working reliably fast. By designing the product originally with that in mind, it not only produced great sales appeal but discovered that this very orientation and intention enabled it to design a quite efficient and low-cost television set. Yet even the most cursory examination of industrial equipment tells a prodigal tale of minuscule attention to the postpurchase repair and maintenance problem. One suspects that the question seldom ever arises. No wonder "service costs so much." No wonder "service takes so much time." No wonder "service is so awful."

In the same fashion, I have elsewhere cited the case of Honeywell, which redesigned its room thermostats to employ far fewer and far more easily replaceable parts and in the process was able to eliminate all its field warehouses and persuade its distributors to carry full parts inventories for faster service both to its customers and to repairmen working on competitive products, for which many Honeywell parts were designed for interchangeability.

EXAMPLES OF SPECIAL
RECENT ACHIEVEMENTS

Ideas and concepts are often easier understood in principle than translated into actuality. Some translations are easy enough to recognize and, in retrospect, easy enough to comprehend as representing the industrialization of service. A few less obvious examples are worth a look.

The paperwork problem

The Transamerica Title Insurance Company receives thousands of title insurance applications each week from numerous small field offices on the West Coast and in the Southwest, Colorado, and Michigan. Clerks and "escrow officers" prepare these applications, for which careful title searches through ancient property records must be made. Escrow officers finally begin preparing preliminary insurance policies, which guarantee the buyer (and protect the lender) against postpurchase claims against the seller, such as faulty property surveys, outstanding liens, unpaid taxes, discovery of subsequent wills that invalidate some seller's presumed title, and the like. The preparation of these preliminary policies requires endless telephone calls, a constant and irregular stream of documentation, and frequent calls for speed, clarification, complaints, and help from the many parties to any single transaction—buyer, seller, listing real estate broker, selling real estate broker, lender, tax collector, surveyor, termite inspector. In all this maelstrom of noise, activity, and push, exact calculations must be made regarding the allocation of credits and debits for pro-rated proportions of remaining taxes, interest, and other assessments. Instructions must be issued regarding each party's remaining duties and where and how these are to be discharged. All this must be done cheerfully, efficiently, rapidly, errorlessly, and for numerous accounts by each escrow officer all day long, all week long. That is, until now.

Now Transamerica has systematically industrialized much

of this complex, pressure-cooker process. By careful analysis of the various functions to be performed and by classifying them by degree of importance (e.g., the extreme importance of thoroughness of title search, and the extreme importance of absolutely error-proof operation in the final "closing" of the transaction and in the final insurance policy), the work was divided into several distinct parts. Instead of having each office person do everything or almost everything, separate installations have been created where some specialists do only title searches, some only the auditing, some only the typing of the "closing" papers, and some only the final policy issuance. Productivity and accuracy improved dramatically. Computerization of the financial calculations and typing helped even more. Meanwhile, in order to guard against the erosion of standards and workmanship that the routinization of work so often produces, systems of work-assignment rotation have been installed and career ladders have been created to give the various specialized workers opportunities for advancement and self-development.

The shoe repair problem

D. Hilston Ryan, product manager of an American package goods company in Europe, grew impatient with a two-week wait to have new heels put on a pair of shoes. He and an associate designed a fast-service shoe repair facility. With no equipment available to meet the needs as they visualized them, they persuaded a manufacturer to produce equipment to their specifications. It was designed to apply new heels and soles on two shoes in less than two minutes. They persuaded the largest department store in Brussels to put their fast-service, while-you-wait, 40-square-foot-shop into the store window on opening day. Lines formed for two blocks. In four years they had 1,400 leased installations in department stores, railroad stations, and supermarkets all over Europe. What was the secret? First, they invented a system to produce speed; not only did they design the equipment, but they also devised its layout, the quality and work-rate standards, the selection and training of workers, the location of inventory relative to the location of the specialized equipment that was used, the type of adhesives and sewing machinery, the seating arrangement for the while-you-wait customers so they could see the work being done, and, of great importance, the low-noise nature of the machines and automatic dust collectors that prevented polluting either the work area or the surrounding store. And the prices charged the customers? Lower, of course.

The selling problem

Few things trouble the business community more than the alleged high and accelerating "cost of selling," especially personal selling. There are, of course, solutions, and I have mentioned some: self-service stores, which simply eliminate the personal selling function; mutual funds, which substitute one sales call for many; packaged travel tours, which substitute pre-planned itineraries for negotiated ones; and, in industrial selling, a plentitude of item and parts catalogs, which facilitate self-service ordering. There is also an enormous explosion of highly sophisticated direct-mail and catalog selling as well as direct-response selling via order forms in newspapers and magazines and via telephone response to television solicitation. In some of these cases the significance of what is being done is that the products and the product lines are a direct consequence of the media that are available for their sale, rather than their having previously existed in a separate life of their own. Thus certain forms of life, casualty, and hospitalization insurance were created specifically for their ability to be sold via the mail, newspapers, or television. The same is true of a large number of music record albums and even of companies, such as the $164-million-a-year K-Tel Corporation, which was specifically organized for television–telephone response merchandising.

Indeed, telephone solicitation and selling has suddenly boomed into one of the great hidden forms of modern selling. In 1975 an average of seven million U.S. consumers a day picked up their telephones to hear someone who wanted to ask them, offer them, or sell them something. Nearly three million of them

—consumers or businesspeople—agreed to listen, and 460,000 completed the offered proposition then and there at an average purchase price of $60, for a total of $28 million per day, or nearly $6 billion a year.

The very first mass-marketing telephone campaign was undertaken a decade ago by Ford Motor Company and executed by Campaign Communications Institute of America, Inc. (CCI), probably the world's foremost firm specializing in offering telephone marketing services. Twenty million telephone calls were made by 15,000 housewives hired and trained to do the job right from their own homes. Following a carefully programmed script they called a million households a day to determine whether their plans made them good prospects for an automobile purchase. On the average, each call took less than one minute. They generated 340,000 leads (during the campaign period, two per day for each of Ford's 23,000 dealer salesmen), 187,000 of which were "valid" in that they proved to be actively interested in buying within six months. Sales attributable to the program were at a campaign cost ($65 per unit), considered by the company far below its many other promotional programs.

Later CCI designed and executed a telephone subscription solicitation campaign for *World* magazine, the new venture of Norman Cousins, the former editor of *The Saturday Review*. Using a very carefully selected call list and, again, a carefully programmed calling approach, telephone solicitation was tested against carefully designed direct mail solicitation. Telephones produced three committed subscriptions for each one produced by mail.[1]

The New York Telephone Company has dozens of specialists and trainers available gratis to its users for advising and training individuals and small groups in improved techniques and procedures of telephone marketing. Telephone marketing, like most things, is a craft that uses tools and techniques that can be learned. What is significant about their recent incarnation is the introduction of carefully controlled and highly structured

[1] The details of how telephone selling has been and can be industrialized are explained in Murray Roman, *Telephone Marketing* (New York: McGraw-Hill Book Co., 1976).

production-line approaches to telephone marketing. Every aspect of the task—caller recruitment, training, call programming, working conditions, and key phrases for getting results—is as carefully planned and executed as what happens on an automotive assembly line. Firms of all kinds in almost all industries increasingly use this medium, usually with the help of professional organizations specializing in its use for such purposes as selling and taking orders, qualifying leads, motivating delinquent accounts, upgrading marginal customers, follow-ups on direct mail, converting inquiries into sales, reactivating old customers, promoting store traffic, finding and screening for new business, soliciting quality credit applications, introducing new products into distribution channels, delivering taped messages to selected audiences, raising funds for institutions or public causes, and, of course, getting out the vote.

With the availability of Wide Area Telephone Service (WATS lines), FX calls, 800 numbers (inbound WATS), and declining long-distance telephone charges (particularly as postal rates and personal-selling costs rise), telephone selling that is organized with production-line rationality has become a major means for the industrialization of various kinds of selling and sales-related communications.

End-use specialization

The computer industry has gone perhaps farther than most in specializing its activities to the requirements of specific uses and industries. Among mainframe producers specialization has centered on selling, programming, and equipment servicing, with salesmen and programmers specializing not by equipment but rather by customer industries and applications. Though it is not usually viewed as such, this division of labor represents the same kind of rational specialization I have cited as productive in other industries. The particular value of citing the computer industry is that it views "service" as a central part of the total product package, in part because, especially in the beginning, prospects and customers were almost totally uninformed about what computers could do and how to use them. Therefore "service" became an essential part of the product itself. Specialization of the sales forces, of the programming, and of the hardware services by end-user industries and by uses produced sales and customer-satisfying results in proportions far beyond those achieved by companies that did not specialize. Specialization is to service what division of labor is to manufacturing: the first step to low-cost, reliable abundance.

Cyrus McCormick pioneered the whole idea, putting demonstration salesmen to work on wheat farms and providing repairmen in the field. DuPont pioneered with applications specialists in the textile and garment industries. In all these cases, the "product" that was offered by the "salesmen" consisted less of what was manufactured in the factory than of what was provided by way of practical help and advice in the field. "Service" *was* the product, and still today in many situations it remains more *the* product than meets the eye. Customers don't buy things, they buy tools to solve problems. Specialists who know the customer's problems are more likely to help fulfill the expectation of solution than those who know only the equipment.

The idea of specialization is actually more common than we are aware. We have become so accustomed to seeing savings and loan institutions standing cheek-by-jowl with commercial banks that we fail to note that each is a separate financial institution organized specifically to specialize in respect to separate markets: savings and loans largely to provide mortgage financing to residential home buyers; commercial banks to provide a wider range of short-term money-related services.

Dozens of examples abound: specialty retail stores (shoes, health and beauty aids, books, sporting goods); specialty service stores (some already mentioned, like shoe repair and muffler replacement, others like dry cleaning, insurance, realty); oil exploration companies like drillers, seismic testing firms, core analysis firms; a vast variety of computer software, computer data-base, and computer processing firms, many specializing in each case in a limited variety of applications; chemical and medical testing firms; investment advisory and fulfillment firms, from those that serve only small individual investors to those that serve only large institutional clients, from those that provide a full range of investment services to boutiques that do only executions. The list is varied and, in recent years, is in explosive expansion. These facts are trying to tell us something. They are trying to say that specialization has a virtue that transcends the simple obvious fact that narrow functional specialization tends to focus energy and attention rather than let them be whirled centrifugally into uncontrolled and uncontrollable bits and pieces where management attention and talent are spread too thin over too much.

About two hundred years ago Adam Smith gave a name to the kind of specialization and concentration I have been talking about. It has traveled in manufacturing and economics ever since under one name: division of labor. The difference in the cases cited above is that this division has become embodied in separate institutions and products, firms specializing in the "labors" into which they divided themselves, and products created around those divided "labors." Thus, what we witness is nothing particularly new. What *is* new is the suggestion that the accidents of evolution which created these institutional specialists and product specializations in service can be explained and contemplated in the theoretical context of what I have called "industrialization." The managerial rationality embodied in the practical imagination we see exercised so effectively everywhere in manufacturing can, given the effort, be applied with similarly munificent results in the service industries. We are only now seeing the practical possibilities of the industrialization of service, which in fact has existed in some form for thousands of years but has recently been pressing forward with accelerating tempo. It's like Lavoisier's discovery in chemistry. Everybody had seen that "air" helps things burn, but until Lavoisier discovered the role of oxygen in combustion, this phenomenon was a mystery. Once explained, this phenomenon that had existed since Prometheus became the foundation of modern chemistry. Now that we understand the underlying reason for the success and growth of these institutions and products, now that we see that they have a common and explicable rationality, this understanding has the potential of having in the world of commerce and industry the revolutionizing impact of Lavoisier's insight in chemistry and life.

So it may very well be with the concept of "industrialization." It is an explanation of what the historic and now accelerating specialization in service is, practically speaking, all about. Man lives not by bread alone, but mostly by catchwords. What he believes and feels in his mind and emotions is more deterministic than what's in his possession. What's in his mind, like love, hate, anger, joy, fear, jealousy, alienation, loyalty, or ideology, religion, causation, consequences—all these are, finally, deterministic. They shape and control his actions. To understand and get into our minds that the kinds of successful specializations of effort in the non-goods-producing sectors of our world that I have so briefly described represent a uniquely organized set of processes, that these are in fact the *industrialization* of activities long thoughtlessly assumed to be uniquely inaccessible to the functional rationality that has produced so much low-cost abundance in the goods-producing sectors of the world's more advanced economies—to recognize and understand this phenomenon for what it practically is—is to introduce a potentially emancipating new cognitive mode and operating style into modern enterprise. "Industrialization in service," like "oxygen in combustion," once it enters our minds, though we have unknowingly lived with it since the beginning of mortal time, can transform how we behave, what we do, and where we go. It can generate liberating new solutions to intractable old problems. It can bring to the increasingly service-dominated economies of the future the same kinds of vaulting advances in productivity and living standards as did the newly created goods-producing factory economies brought to the world in the past.

4

Differentiation—of Anything

There is no such thing as a commodity. All goods and services can be differentiated and usually are. Though the usual presumption is that this is true more of consumer goods than of industrial goods and services, the opposite is the actual case.

The only exception to this proposition is in the minds of people who profess that exception. In the market place differentiation is everywhere. Everybody—whether producer, fabricator, seller, broker, agent, merchant—engages in a constant effort to distinguish his offering in his favor from all others. This is true even of those who produce, deal in, or buy primary metals, grains, chemicals, plastics, or money.

In fabricated consumer and industrial goods, competitive distinction is visibly sought via distinctive product features, some visually or measurably identifiable, some cosmetically implied, and some rhetorically claimed by reference to real or suggested hidden attributes that promise results or values different from those of competitors.

So too with consumer and industrial services—what I shall call, to be accurate, "intangibles."

Though it is true that on the commodities exchanges dealers in metals, grains, pork bellies, and the like trade in totally undifferentiated generic products, what they "sell" is the claimed distinction of their execution—how well they make transactions in behalf of their clients, how responsive they are to inquiries, the clarity and quickness of their confirmations, and so on. In short, the "offered" product is differentiated, though the "generic" product (say, Treasury Bill futures, gold bullion, or No. 2 winter wheat) is identical.

It is precisely when the generic product is undifferentiated that the "offered" product makes the difference in getting customers, and the "delivered" product in keeping them. When the enormously knowledgeable senior partner of a well-known Chicago brokerage firm appeared at New York banks in a tight-fitting lime-green polyester suit and Gucci shoes soliciting trading business for financial instrument futures, the outcome was predictably poor. The unintended offering implied by his sartorial appearance contradicted the intended offering of his carefully prepared presentation. No wonder that Thomas Watson the elder insisted so uncompromisingly that his salesmen be "properly" attired in their famous IBM "uniform." Though clothes may not make the man, they may help make the sale. And if they do, the customer is buying something beyond the generic product that the salesman offers. That is what is meant by "differentiation."

The usual presumption about so-called undifferentiated commodities is that they are exceedingly price sensitive. A fractionally lower price gets the business. That's seldom true except in the imaginary world of economics textbooks. In the actual world of real markets, nothing is exempt from other considerations, even when price competition is virulent. The fact that price differences are, prima facie, measurable becomes the usual, and usually false, basis for asserting their powerful primacy.

73

Price is, of course, powerful. But to be powerful is not automatically to be sufficient, no matter how narrowly price negotiations get hardened or to what minuscule fractions price bids are driven.

During periods of sustained surplus, excess capacity, or unrelieved price wars, when all attention seems firmly riveted on nothing but price, it is precisely because price is so visibly objective (i.e., measurable) and so potentially devastating in its effects that it deflects attention from the possibilities for successful extrication from ravaging price competition. So compelling are the price pressures that other possibilities get proportionately slighted. Nor are these "other possibilities," even in the short run, confined simply to "nonprice competition," such as harder personal selling, intensified or enhanced advertising, or what's loosely called more or better "services."

To see fully what these "other possibilities" are, it is useful first to remind ourselves more firmly exactly what a product is.

WHAT IS A PRODUCT?

Some things are easy enough to see and have been often noted. Products may be tangible and intangible. Often they are combinations of both. An automobile is not simply a tangible machine for movement, visibly or measurably differentiated by design, size, color, options, horsepower, or miles per gallon. It is also a complex symbol denoting status, taste, rank, achievement, aspiration, and, these days, being "smart"—that is, buying economy rather than display. But the customer buys even more than these. The enormous efforts of the auto companies to cut the time between placement and delivery of an order and to select, train, supervise, motivate, and enhance their dealerships suggest that these too are integral parts of "the product" people buy and are therefore ways by which they may be differentiated.

In the same way a computer is not simply a machine for data storage, processing, calculation, or retrieval. It is also an operating system with special software protocols for use and special accompanying possibilities for and promises of maintenance and repair.

Carbon fibers are chemical additives that enhance flexuous stiffness, reduce weight, fight fatigue and corrosion, and cut fabrication costs when combined with certain other materials. But they have no value for an inexperienced user without the heavy design and applications help that only the experienced seller can provide.

Securities underwriters deliver money to the issuers but also promises to the buyers. The promises are carefully packaged in prospectuses of awesome length and detail, only part of whose contents are prescribed by law. The rest is a portentous advertisement for the offering, on the tombstone page of which the members of the underwriting syndicate are listed in a ritual hierarchical order that itself represents a constant battle for advertised image supremacy by the syndicate members themselves. As in the case of thousand-page major-contract proposals to the National Aeronautics and Space Administration or five-page consulting proposals to industrial clients, "the product" is a promise whose commercial substance resides as much in the proposer's carefully curried reputation (or "image") and in the proposal's meticulous packaging as it does in its substantive content.

When the substantive content—the generic product—of competing vendors is scarcely differentiable, sales power migrates to all other differentiating ways in which buyers are likely to be influenced. In this regard there is scant substantive difference between what's done by Morgan Stanley & Co., by Lockheed, McKinsey & Co., and by Revlon. Though each will, in public, vigorously proclaim commanding generic distinctions vis-à-vis competitors, in practice each is profoundly preoccupied with packaging, that is, representing itself as unique. And, indeed, each may be unique. But its uniqueness in relation to its competitors resides precisely in things that transcend its generic offerings. All four offer "products" that extend beyond what is at their generic core. The reason is clear enough: The generic core seldom has competitive viability by itself. It must be differentiated from competitive offerings, because people understandably respond to differentiation, and they respond differently to different kinds of differentiation.

When I say "people" respond, I mean nobody is exempt, not even the chief executives of the world's largest and best-managed corporations or the Ph.D. scientists in their laboratories. "One eminent [U.S. investment banking] house has entrances on two streets, with a different set of stationery printed for each entrance. One door is intended to be more exclusive than the other, and a visitor supposedly can tell the firm's assessment of his importance by the entrance indicated on the letterhead of the stationery he receives."[1] Obviously, the distinctions being made are selling devices based on the assumption that VIP treatment of some visitors at reception will convince them that they will get a VIP product.

As for how Ph.D. corporate laboratory scientists make vendor decisions, a carefully controlled study of purchasing behavior regarding complex new industrial materials showed that

> . . . technically sophisticated technical personnel seem to be influenced by the seller's reputation to a point that is unexpectedly higher than the influence of that reputation on such technically less sophisticated personnel as purchasing agents. . . . In . . . trying to sell such products to technically trained personnel it may not be wise to rely so unevenly on the product's inherent virtues and on making strong technical product presentations. Technical personnel are not human computers whose purchasing and product-specification decisions are based on cold calculations and devoid of less rigorously rational influences.[2]

People buy products (whether purely tangible products, purely intangible products, or hybrids of the two) in order to solve problems. Products are problem-solving tools. If the buyer won't buy for lack of help in design and application, it's not a product, because it does not fulfill a problem-solving need. Certainly it is incomplete. If he won't buy because it is styled unsuitably, its delivery is uncertain, its sales terms are un-

[1] This is from page 147 of a highly prescient study on the workings of image and other forms of competition among investment-banking firms, Samuel L. Hayes, III, "Investment Banking: Power Structure in Flux," *Harvard Business Review,* March/April 1971, pp. 136–52.
[2] Theodore Levitt, *Industrial Purchasing Behavior: A Study of Communications Effects* (Boston: Division of Research, Graduate School of Business Administration, Harvard University, 1965), pp. 26–27.

acceptable, its maintenance difficult, the salesperson is officious, the proposal has misspellings or lacks clarity, the store smells, or the supplier's general reputation is questionable or only slightly inferior to that of another—if all or any of these keep the prospect from buying, then clearly the prospect thinks of a product as more than the generic engineering "thing" that's made in the factory, the generic benefit bundle that's described in the proposal, or the generic item that's on display.

A product is, to the potential buyer, a complex cluster of value satisfactions. The generic "thing" or "essence" is not itself the product. It is merely, as in poker, the table stake, the minimum necessary at the outset to allow its producer into the game. But it's only a "chance," only a right to enter play. Once entry is actually attained, the outcome depends on a great many other things. Mostly it depends on how the entrant plays the game, rather than on the table stake (the generic product) that entitles one to play. In business, as in poker, there is competition, but in business it is for the patronage of solvent customers. Customers attach value to products in proportion to the perceived ability of those products to help solve their problems. Hence a product has meaning only from the viewpoint of the buyer or the ultimate user. All else is derivative. Only the buyer or user can assign value, because value can reside only in the benefits he wants or perceives.

Nothing demonstrates this more clearly than the supreme clarity with which the Detroit auto companies buy sheet steel. Detroit buys to exceedingly tight technical specifications, but it specifies more than the qualities of the steel itself. It also specifies a vast variety of delivery conditions and flexibilities, price and payment conditions, reordering responsiveness, and the like. Employing multiple suppliers, the Detroit companies shift from year to year the proportions of steel they buy from their various suppliers on the basis of elaborate grading systems by which they measure the performance of their suppliers on each of the specified conditions.

Clearly Detroit views "the product" as more than the specified sheet steel alone. It buys a bundle of value specifications of which sheet steel, the generic product, is only a small proportion. If other parts of the product it buys—the delivery conditions and flexibilities, for example—are not fulfilled, or if they are fulfilled erratically, grudgingly, or only partially, the customer is not getting "the product" he expects. If one supplier gets, on a ten-point scale, a lot of sixes and sevens for the dimensions on which he gets graded, while another supplier gets mostly nines and tens, next year the latter will get more of the business. His "product" is better; he delivers more value. Although the steel is absolutely identical, the customer knows that "the products" are different, and the difference, in all probability, is greater than the housewife is able to discern between coffees from Maxwell House and Folger. Detroit sees with supreme clarity that No. 302, 72-inch hot-rolled strip carbon steel is not a commodity. It is a measurably differentiated product. It is never just steel, wheat, subassemblies, investment banking, engineering consultancy, industrial maintenance, newsprint, or even 99 percent pure isopropanol.

What a product is in its customer-getting and customer-satisfying entirety can be managed. But it seldom is. Things just happen, often entirely too serendipitously. To see how it can be managed, it is helpful to look in some graphic detail at how it might be visualized.

Visually, one can describe a product as having the range of possibilities shown in Figure 1, which is explained below.

The generic product

The "generic product" is the rudimentary substantive "thing" without which there is no chance to play the game of market participation. It is the "table stake" of the game. For the steel producer it is the steel itself. In the case of a bank, it is loanable funds. For a realtor, it is "for sale" properties. For a machine tools maker it is the lathe, milling, shaping or other equipment in whose production he may specialize. For a retailer it is a store with a certain mix of vendables. For a lawyer it's having passed the bar exam. For a producer of chemical feed stocks it is those feed stocks themselves.

FIGURE 1. THE TOTAL PRODUCT CONCEPT

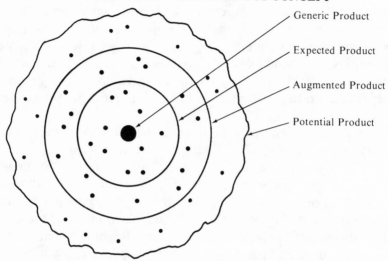

Note: The dots inside each ring represent specific activities or tangible attributes. For example, inside the "Expected Product" are delivery conditions, installation services, postpurchase services, maintenance, spare parts, training, packaging convenience, and the like.

To be a producer of chemical feed stocks, say, benzene (the "Generic Product" depicted by the solid black center in Figure 1), is not automatically to be a seller of benzene, certainly not a successful seller. The customer, as we saw in the Detroit example, expects more than the generic product when he pays, nominally, for that product. Unless his other expectations are minimally fulfilled, there will be no sale. And if it is not sold, there is no "it." Commercially speaking, there is no product when what there "is" has no takers. The customer expects more.

The expected product

Figure 1 represents the "Expected Product" as everything inside the smallest circle, including the "Generic Product." This represents the customer's minimal expectations. Though these vary by customers, conditions, industries, and the like, every customer has minimal purchase conditions that exceed the generic product itself. Benzene must not simply be "priced right" but must also be delivered "right," which can refer to minimal quantities and schedules and to specific locations in varying amounts at specified times. Payment terms have to be "right." Depending on the customer, technical support or help has to be "right."

The same general principles clearly apply to everything everywhere. A shabby brokerage office may cost the realtor access to a customer for his "for sale" properties. Even though the lawyer performed magnificently in the bar exam and occupies offices of prudential elegance, his abrasive personality may put off a potential client. The machine tools might have the most sophisticated of numerical controls tucked tightly behind an impressively designed panel, but certain prospects may not buy, in spite of all else being "right," because the machine's output tolerances are more precise than necessary or usable. The customer may actually expect and want less. For him, more is not better, not even at a competitive price.

Not even in such a putatively homogeneous product as wheat does the customer buy only the generic product itself. Indeed there are in the United States three kinds of wheat: winter wheat, which represents about 30 percent of U.S. production; spring wheat; and so-called specialty wheats, like durum. Durum itself comes in its own subspecialties, the most abundance of which is semolina, which is used almost exclusively for making pastas. About 90 percent of all U.S. durum is grown in three counties in Eastern North Dakota. Yet prices vary substantially, even for identical grades of semolina. The county elevator operators to whom most semolina farmers sell will pay premiums or take discounts from previously agreed-to or currently quoted prices, depending on the results of protein and moisture tests made on each delivery. The wheat users ("buyers"), like Prince Spaghetti Company, make additional tests for farina and gluten content, which result in additional price adjustments. Premiums and discounts for quality differences in a given year have been known to vary from the futures price on the commodity exchanges by amounts greater than the futures price fluctuations themselves during that year.

There are also variations in the expected product. Elevator operators require bulk delivery in truckload quantities. Before elevator operators installed their own truck-lifting facilities, delivery generally had to be in trucks equipped with their own hydraulic lifts to facilitate dumping. In recent years many of the larger farmers have installed their own storage elevators. Using very large trailer trucks, they bypass county elevators for direct shipment to the receiving elevators of large users. Besides avoiding middleman storage discounts, this gives them better access to quality premiums paid by buyers.

Similarly county elevator operators in the Great Plains increasingly try to organize themselves to take advantage of unit-train shipments to the Gulf Coast. Single offerings of ten-carload shipments qualify for substantial rail tariff discounts. This affects the quantities and schedules by which county elevators prefer to buy and take delivery from growers, which in turn affects how the growers manage their delivery capabilities and schedules.

Thus, not even specific types or grades of wheat are a commodity. They can be, and are generally expected by their buyers to be, differentiated. Clearly, when we know enough about a business it becomes clear that its "product" is much more than what's generically at the core of what's expected by the customer and offered by the seller.

When the customer expects more than the generic product, the generic product can be sold only if those expectations are met. The different means by which competing sellers seek to fulfill these expectations distinguish their offerings from one another. In this way, differentiation follows expectations.

The augmented product

But differentiation is not exhausted merely by giving the customer what he expects. What he expects may be augmented by offering him more than what he thinks he needs or has become accustomed to expect. When the selling manufacturer of, say, computers implants a software diagnostic module inside his computers which automatically locates the source of failure or breakdown (as some now do), that seller has augmented the product beyond what was required or even expected by the buyer. When a securities brokerage firm includes with its customers' monthly statements a current balance sheet for each customer and an analysis of sources and disposition of funds, that firm has augmented its product beyond what was required or even expected by the buyer. When a manufacturer of health and beauty aids offers warehouse-management advice and training programs for the employees of its distributors, that firm too has augmented its product beyond what was required or even expected by the buyer.

These voluntary or unprompted "augmentations" to the expected product are depicted in Figure 1 by the band that surrounds the "Expected Product." The "augmented product" comprises what's in this band plus everything that it surrounds. The process of providing these augmentations can, in time, educate the buyer about what is reasonable for him to expect from the seller. Just as one seller's more attractive delivery or payment terms raise the customer's expectations from all sellers, so also do all the other ways in which sellers surround the generic and the expected product with an expanding variety of customer-benefiting attributes designed to attract and hold customers. Again, customer expectations rise to what has been shown to customers to be possible.

The size and content of a product therefore consists, first, of the generic product and the customer-originated expectations regarding the conditions that must be fulfilled in order for him to buy it, and of the seller-originated augmentations with which additional competitive advantage is sought. Augmentations are a means of product differentiation. Nearly everybody employs them, though they are seldom developed as part of a conscious or systematic program of product differentiation.

Not all customers for all products and under all circumstances can be attracted by an ever widening bundle of these differentiating "value satisfactions." Some customers may prefer lower prices to more augmentations. Some cannot use certain offered augmentations. For example:

—A retailer who is large enough to take store-door delivery rather than buy from a distributor or operate his own distribution center cannot use or benefit from the kinds of distribution-center operating or training aids mentioned above.

—In the case of maturing products, the passage of time may result in the buyer's becoming so thoroughly expert in the use of the "generic product" that he no longer needs or wants applications or engineering support. Thus the rapid growth of independent steel distribution centers has paralleled the declining need of steel-using customers for mill-originated applications help. Meanwhile, independent steel distribution centers, whose "product" has always been distinguished from the mill-originated product by greater delivery speed on standard grades and sizes, a wider item mix, and ability to handle small orders, have augmented their product by doing more minor fabricating and adding certain specialty-steel applications services.

The rule can be laid down that the more successfully a seller expands the market by teaching and helping customers to use his product, the more vulnerable the seller becomes to the loss of those customers. When a prospect no longer needs the help that converted him into a customer, he becomes free to shop around for things he values more than that help. Often this is price. But the booming U.S. growth of independent steel distribution and fabrication centers suggests that price is not the only thing that attracts and holds the buyer.

It is precisely when the buyer has become less dependent on the technical help or brand support of the originating supplier that greater attention may be beneficially focused on a systematic program of finding customer-benefitiating and therefore customer-keeping product augmentations. It is also a time when increasing effort should be focused on possible cost and price reductions. Thus arises the irony of product maturity: Precisely when price competition gets more severe and therefore cost reduction becomes more important is when one is also likely to benefit by incurring the additional costs of special new product augmentations.

The augmented product is uniquely a condition of relatively mature markets or of relatively experienced or sophisticated customers. Not that more experienced or sophisticated customers cannot benefit or will not respond to augmented offerings; but when a customer knows or thinks he knows everything and can do anything, it is up to the seller to test those assumptions lest he be condemned to the purgatory of price competition alone. The way to "test" the customer's assumption that he no longer needs or wants all or any part of the augmented product is to consider what's potentially possible to offer.

The potential product

The "potential product" consists of everything potentially feasible to attract and hold customers. Whereas the "augmented product" means everything that has been or is being done, the "potential product" refers to what may remain to be done, that is, what is possible.

What may be possible is not strictly a matter of what is purely imaginable on the basis of what is known or knowable about customers and competitors. It generally depends heavily on changing conditions. That is why people in business so seldom any longer greet each other with the old rhetorical question, How's business? Instead they ask the more substantively information-seeking question, What's new? That helps describe what has changed, and this helps define the potential product with which to compete more effectively under the changed conditions. When American independent steel distributors saw the declining reliance of steel users on mill-originated technical support, they began buying increasingly from overseas mills, expanded their facilities to carry larger inventories for even faster deliveries, and increased their fabrication capabilities. The response of American mills was to integrate forward by expanding their own distribution and fabrication centers, in some cases actually buying part of their requirements from competing overseas mills.

All this was succinctly described in 1976 by Professor E. Raymond Corey of the Harvard Business School:

1. ". . . the form of a product is a variable, not a given, in developing market strategy. Products are planned and developed to serve markets."
2. ". . . the 'product' is what the product does; it is the total package of benefits the customer receives when he buys. . . . Even though a product might, in the most narrow sense, be indifferentiable, an individual supplier may differentiate his product from competitive offerings through service, product availability, and brand image. And differentiation in one respect or another is the basis for developing a market franchise."
3. ". . . the product, in this broad sense, will have different meaning to different customers. This consideration is important with regard to both market selection and pricing."[3]

This final point about "market selection and pricing" leads us to another form of differentiation, for which all that's been said till now is prologue.

DIFFERENTIATION VIA MARKETING MANAGEMENT

The way a company manages its marketing can become the most powerful form of differentiation. When Professor Corey writes of the options regarding "market selection and pricing" available to sellers, he refers, in effect, to how the marketing process is managed. Indeed, that may be how industrial-product

[3] E. Raymond Corey, *Industrial Marketing: Cases and Concepts* (Englewood Cliffs, N.J., Prentice-Hall, 1976), pp. 40–41.

companies vary most from one to another and therefore may constitute their most important forms of differentiation.

Brand management and product management are managerial tools of marketing that have demonstrable advantages over simple catchall functional modes of management. The same is true of market management, a system widely employed when a specific industrial tangible or intangible is used by many different kinds of industries. Putting somebody in charge of a product that's bought and used essentially in the same way by a large segment of the total market (as in the case, say, of packaged detergents sold through retail channels) or in charge of a specific market for a product that's bought and used in essentially different ways in different industries (as in the case, say, of isopropanol sold directly to manufacturers or indirectly via distributors) so clearly focuses attention, responsibility, and effort that clear competitive advantage generally goes to firms so organized.

A great many generically undifferentiated consumer goods are operationally differentiated by means of branding, packaging, advertising, at times stylized features, and even pricing. Differentiation by pricing is, however, derivative. If nothing else is done (at the minimum, with packaging), price differentiation alone generally fails.

The list of highly differentiated consumer products that not so long ago were sold as essentially undifferentiated or minimally differentiated commodities is long: coffee, soap, flour, beer, sugar, salt, oatmeal, pickles, frankfurters, rice, bananas, chickens, pineapples, potatoes, and lots more. Among consumer intangibles, in recent years there has been an intensification of brand or vendor differentiation in banking, insurance of all kinds, auto rentals, credit cards, stock brokerage, airlines, travel agencies, realtors, beauticians, entertainment parks, small-loan companies, mutual funds, bond funds, and lots more. Among consumer hybrids the same thing has occurred: fast foods, theme restaurants, opticians, food retailers, and specialty retailers in a burgeoning variety of categories—jewelry, sporting goods, books, health and beauty aids, pants and jeans, musical records and cassettes, auto supplies and parts, ice cream shops, home improvement centers, and lots more.

In each of these cases, especially those of consumer tangibles, the general assumption among the less informed is that their competitive distinction rests largely on packaging and advertising. Even substantive differences in the generic products are presumed to be so minimal that what really count are the ads and the packages.

This presumption is one of the most palpably wrong of all the many wrong presumptions that parade so abundantly as wisdom among even insiders in the affected industries. It is not simply their ads or packages that account for the preeminence of General Foods and Proctor & Gamble in so many of their product categories. Nor is it their superior generic products that explain the greater successes of IBM, Xerox, ITT, and Texas Instruments. If either were so, executive recruiters would be less successful in attracting raw material to these outstanding companies.

Their real distinction lies heavily in how they manage. In the case of P&G, General Foods, IBM, and Xerox, it is especially in how they manage marketing. The amount of careful but hidden analysis, control, and field work that characterizes their management of marketing is masked by the enormous visibility of their advertising or presumed generic product uniqueness.

The branded grocery products companies advertise heavily, just as the auto companies do. But they don't have franchised dealers. They have wholesale and retail "distributors," and, depending on which firm we talk about, they work as hard and as closely with their distributors as do the auto companies. Indeed, often they work with them even harder, because their "distributors" handle many competing brands, and the distribution channels are longer and more complex.

Most retail grocery stores handle a number of more or less competing brands of the same generic (or functionally undifferentiated) product. There are more than two dozen national brands of powdered laundry detergent. They are sold to retail buyers mostly in supermarkets or small convenience stores, which get them either from a supermarket chain warehouse or the warehouse of a cooperative wholesaler, a voluntary wholesaler, or an independent wholesaler. Each of these warehouses generally carries a full line of competing brands. Though the national brands try through advertising and promotion to create consumer "pull," they are heavily involved as well in trying to create retailer and wholesaler "push." At retail they regularly seek more advantageous shelf space and more advertising support from the retailer directly. At wholesale they do other things. Some years ago General Foods did a massive study of materials handling in distribution warehouses, making its results and recommendations available to the trade through a carefully trained crew of specialists who helped the trade implement those recommendations. The object, obviously, was to curry special favor with the distributive trades for General Foods' products. The company did something similar for retailers: It made a major study of retail space profitability and then offered retailers a new way of space-profitability accounting. The assumption was that if they helped retailers better manage their space, retailers would favor General Foods products in their merchandising activities. The program was specifically aimed at supermarkets.

At the same time Pillsbury devised Creative Marketing Systems, a program designed specifically to help small convenience stores to operate and compete more effectively. The object was, of course, to obtain preferential "push" treatment for Pillsbury products in these stores.

There is, moreover, a continuous process of improved logistical and material-handling interfacing between suppliers, distributors, and retailers. Deliveries are often scheduled to arrive at specific hours and dates, much as they are for auto assembly plants by parts suppliers. The form in which they are delivered —pallets, dollies, bulk, and the like—are often customized, and retailer preference as to particular shippers are quickly honored. All this is in the service of gaining preference over competitors. The "product" that's bought for the home at retail is one thing, but the same thing is an equally different "product" bought by the store, and still different when bought by the wholesaler. In each case the originating seller tries to achieve some positive differentiating advantages over his competitors.

Nor does the matter stop there. When Heinz packages, sells, and delivers ketchup to institutional purveyors who supply hospitals, restaurants, hotels, prisons, schools, and nursing homes, it not only operates otherwise than when it deals with cooperative wholesalers but also seeks to operate differently in some advantage-producing fashion from Hunt Foods when it deals with the same purveyors. An example of how far this can go is provided by General Foods, whose Institutional Food Service Division some years ago provided elaborate theme-meal recipes for schools, "safari" meals that included such delectables as "Groundnut Soup Uganda," and "Fish Mozambique." General Foods provided "decorations to help you go native" in the cafeteria, including travel posters, Congo face masks, pith helmets, tiger tails, lotus garlands, and paper monkeys. These were merchandised by and through the purveyors in order to raise demand for the General Foods products in the menus.

Such examples abound in consumer-goods marketing, although the visible superstructure of heavy advertising and special packaging often leads people engaged in other industries to the erroneous view that the latter is what marketing is most about in consumer goods, that that's mostly how they differentiate.

It's not. That's only what's easily seen. What's not so easily seen is how they manage their marketing. All four companies referred to before (General Foods, P&G, IBM, Xerox) are organized along product or brand-management lines for their major generic products, and in the case of IBM and Xerox these are complemented with market managers as well. What differentiates them from others is how well they manage marketing, not just what is visibly marketed. It is the *process,* not just the product, that is uniquely differentiated.

Consider the case of a large manufacturer of isopropyl alcohol, commonly called isopropanol. It is a moderately simple, totally undifferentiated generic product chemically synthesized via a well-known process from gas recovered in petroleum refining. It comes in two grades: crude, which is 9 percent water, and refined, which is 1 percent water. In 1970, 1.9 million pounds were produced in the United States, 43 percent being used as a feed stock to make acetone, which had a variety of uses including as a solvent for protective coatings, as a process solvent, and in manufacturing plastics, synthetic fibers, phar-maceuticals, and other chemicals. Isopropanol is also used to make intermediate chemicals such as isopropyl acetate and iso-propyl amine, which are used to make plastics, synthetic fibers, and paints and other protective coatings. Isopropanol is also used in large amounts for making various lacquers and protec-tive coatings. Some of it is used by its producers themselves, who are vertically integrated to make some of the above prod-ucts but also sell it directly to other manufacturers and to dis-tributors.

Because of the introduction of the new cumene process for making acetone, in 1970 isopropanol was in vast oversupply. Prices were deeply depressed and were expected to remain so for some five years until demand caught up to the supply. One of the larger isopropanol producers in 1970 sold 310 million pounds of acetone and isopropanol into the so-called merchant market—that is, direct to a large number and variety of manu-facturers. The distribution of these sales was represented by the Sales Department as follows:

Industry or Use	Million lb
Acetone	124
Other intermediates	20
Agri-biochemical	31
Coatings	86
Other	49
Total	310

Though the so-called prevailing prices per pound for both acetone and isopropanol were exceedingly low (as low as 4 cents for acetone and 6.7 cents for isopropanol), a careful analysis of this producer's invoices showed wide variations around these prices for sales made to different customers on precisely the same days. Two possible conclusions follow: (1) Not all buyers were identically informed about what indeed were the "prevail-ing" prices on each of those days, and (2) not all buyers were equally price sensitive. Further analysis showed that these price variations tended often to cluster by industry category and by customer size, but not geographically. A further breakdown of industry categories revealed yet other "price segments." Different kinds of coatings manufacturers exhibited different clusterings of prices they had paid. There were substantial relative differences in prices paid between most agricultural chemical producers and different types of biochemical producers. The category called "other" showed many different price clusters.

Had the marketing process been managed reasonably properly, there might have been a product manager who would have requested the types of analyses the results of which I've just mentioned. Inevitably, the revealed differences in invoice prices and price clusterings would have led a moderately intelligent and inquisitive product manager to ask:

1. Who seem to be the least price aware or price sensitive among the various industry user sectors to which we sell? What is their size distribution? Who exactly are the companies?
2. Who are the most and the least vendor "loyal"—that is, who buy regularly from us, regardless of price fluctuations? Why? And who buy from us occasionally, largely apparently because of price?
3. Who can use or needs our applications help most? Who least?
4. Who will respond most to our offer for help?
5. Where and with whom might we selectively raise prices? Selectively hold prices?
6. How should all this be communicated to the sales organization and be employed to manage the sales forces?

Consider the economics of the situation. Suppose that by careful management of the sales force these generically undifferentiated products (acetone and isopropanol) had been sold largely to the less informed or less price-sensitive industry sectors or customers? Suppose each of the broadly defined customer segments had yielded higher prices of as little as .1 cents per pound, .2 cents per pound, or .5 cents per pound? What would have been the immediate cash contribution to our company? The following table suggests some answers.

Industry or Use	Million lb	Additional Cash Contributions, by Price Premiums		
		.1¢	.2¢	.5¢
Acetone	124	$124,000	$248,000	$620,000
Other intermediates	20	20,000	40,000	100,000
Agri-biochemical	31	31,000	62,000	155,000
Coatings	86	86,000	172,000	430,000
Other	49	49,000	98,000	245,000
Total	310	$310,000	$620,000	$1,550,000
If 50% had been sold at the premiums		$155,000	$310,000	$775,000
If 10% had been sold at the premiums		$31,000	$62,000	$155,000

Thus if only 10 percent of total sales had been sold for only one-tenth of a penny more than they were, the pretax contribution would have risen $31,000. If 50 percent of sales had been raised by this minuscule amount, it would have yielded an extra $155,000; $310,000 if 50 percent had been raised by .2 of one cent.

Given the analysis of markets and users explained above, some such increases seem highly probable. How much would it have been worth to expand the market analysis function into an on-the-spot, on-line activity that would have guided the sales organization to get these results? Obviously a lot. By doing precisely this, this producer would have differentiated itself from its competitors in a manner that one could reasonably expect would have yielded highly profitable differential results.

It is precisely this and related kinds of attention to marketing details that characterizes the work of product managers and market managers. Among producers of generically undifferentiated products—particularly products sold as ingredients to industrial customers—*the management of the marketing process can itself be a powerful differentiating device.* This device is constantly and assiduously employed in the better-managed branded consumer packaged goods companies, which are so often falsely viewed as differentiating only what they sell, not how they manage what is sold.

Differentiation is possible everywhere, and one of its more powerful hidden forms is how the marketing process is managed. In this may reside for many companies, especially those selling what they think of as commodities, the opportunity to escape the commodity trap.

5

Marketing Intangible Products and Product Intangibles

Is the marketing of "services" different from the marketing of "goods"?

The answer, as in most things, is equivocal: The principles may be the same, but translation into practice may be profoundly different.

To understand the difference, it helps to change the words we use. Instead of talking of "goods" and of "services," it is better to talk of "tangibles" and "intangibles." To understand the distinction is to appreciate its practicality.

Tangible products can usually be directly experienced—seen, touched, smelled, tasted, and tested. Often this can be done before you buy. You can test drive a car, smell the perfume, work the numerical controls of a milling machine, inspect the seller's steam-generating installation elsewhere, pretest an extruding machine. Intangible products (like transportation, freight forwarding, insurance, repair, consulting, computer soft-

94

ware, investment banking, brokerage, education, health care, accounting) can seldom be experienced or tested in advance.

The significance of modern times is, however, that even the most tangible and experienceable of products cannot, in fact, be reliably tested or experienced in advance. To inspect a vendor's steam-generating plant in advance at another location and to study thoroughly his detailed proposal and design are not enough. Like a successful computer installation, a great deal more is involved than product features and physical installation alone. Though a customer may "buy" a product whose generic tangibility (like the computer or the steam plant) is as palpable as the primeval rocks, and though he may have agreed after great study and extensive negotiation to a cost that runs into the millions of dollars, the process of getting it built on time, installed, and then smoothly operational involves an awful lot more than the generic tangible product itself. What's more crucially at stake are usually a lot of complex, slippery, and difficult intangibles that can make or break the "product's" success. That's true even of mature consumer goods like dishwashing machines, shampoos, and frozen pizza. If a shampoo is not used as prescribed or a pizza not heated as intended, the results can be terrible. So it makes sense to say that all products are in some crucial respects intangible. No matter how diligently designed in advance and carefully constructed in the factory, if installed or used "incorrectly" they'll fail or disappoint in use. The significance of all this for their marketing can be profound.

There are exceptions to the distinctions that separate tangible from intangible products. You can't taste in advance or even see sardines in a can or soap in a box. This is commonly so of frequently purchased moderate- to low-priced consumer goods. To make buyers more comfortable and confident about tangibles that can't be pretested, companies go beyond the literal promises of specifications, advertisements, and labels to provide reassurance. Packaging is a common tool. Pickles are put into see-through glass jars, cookies into cellophane-windowed boxes, canned goods get strong appetite-appealing pictures on the labels, architects make elaborately enticing renderings, and proposals to NASA are packaged in binders that match the craftsmanship of Tyrolean leatherworkers. In all cases the idea is to provide reassuring tangible (in these examples, visual) surrogates for what's promised but can't be more directly experienced till consumption.

Exceptions in intangible products are also frequent. You *can* see a hotel room before you rent and use it. You *can* study a computer software program, and samples of its output, before you buy. But, more than even canned goods, intangible products force buyers to depend on surrogates to assess what they're likely to get. They can look at gloriously glossy pictures of elegant rooms in distant resort hotels set by the shimmering sea. They can consult current users to see how well a software program performs or how well the investment banker or the oil well drilling contractor performs; they can ask experienced customers regarding engineering firms, trust companies, lobbyists, professors, surgeons, prep schools, hair stylists, consultants, repair shops, industrial maintenance firms, shippers, franchisers, general contractors, funeral directors, caterers, environment management firms, construction companies, and on and on.

When prospective customers can't taste, test, feel, smell, or watch the product in operation in advance, what they are asked to buy are, simply, promises of satisfaction. Even tangible, testable, feelable, smellable products are, before they're bought, largely promises.

Satisfaction later in consumption or use can seldom be quite the same as earlier in trial or promise. Some promises promise more than others. It depends on product features, design, degree of tangibility, type of promotion, price, and differences in what customers hope to accomplish with what they buy. Of some products less is expected than what is explicitly or symbolically promised. The right kind of eye shadow properly applied may promise to transform you into an irresistible tigress in the night. But not even the most eager buyer literally believes the metaphor. Still, the metaphor makes the sale. Neither do you literally expect the proposed new corporate headquarters, so artfully rendered by the winning architect, automatically to produce all those cheerfully productive employees the renderings show lounging with casual elegance at lunch in the verdant courtyard.

Yet the metaphor helps win the assignment. When prospective customers can't taste, test, feel, smell, watch, or properly try the promised product in advance, the necessity of metaphorical reassurances to the marketing effort becomes amplified. Promises, being intangible, have to be tangibilized in their presentation, hence the tigress and the lounging employees. Metaphors and similes become surrogates for the tangibility that cannot be provided or experienced in advance.

This accounts for the solid, somber, Edwardian decor of downtown law offices; for the prudentially elegant and orderly public offices of investment banking houses; for the confidently articulate consultants in dark vested suits; for engineering and project proposals in "executive" type and leather bindings; for the elaborate pictorial documentation of the performance virtuosity of newly offered machine controls. It explains why insurance companies pictorially offer "a piece of the rock," put you under a "blanket of protection," under an "umbrella," or in "good hands."

Not even tangible products are exempt from the necessity of using symbol and metaphor. A computer terminal has to look "right." It has to be "packaged" to convey an impression of reliable modernity—based on the assumption that prospective buyers will translate appearance into confidence about performance. In that respect, the marketing ideas behind the "packaging" of a $1-million computer, a $2-million jet engine, and a half-million-dollar numerically controlled milling machine are scarcely different from the marketing ideas behind the "packaging" of a $50 electric shaver or a $1.50 tube of lipstick.

Common sense tells us, and research confirms, that people use appearances to make judgments about realities. It matters little whether the products are high-priced or low-priced, whether they are technically complex or simple, whether the buyers are supremely sophisticated in the technology of what's being considered or just plain ignorant, or whether they buy for themselves or for their employers. Everybody always depends to some extent on appearances, on external impressions.

Nor is the importance of impressions limited only to the "generic" product itself—that is, to the technical offering, such as the speed, versatility, and precision of the lathe, the color and creaminess of the lipstick, or the taste and size of the lobster thermadore. Consider investment banking. No matter how thorough and persuasive a firm's recommendations and assurances about a proposed underwriting, no matter how pristine its reputation for integrity and performance, somehow the financial vice president of the billion-dollar client corporation would feel better had the bank's representative not been quite so youthful and apple-cheeked. The offered products will be judged in part by who personally offers it—not just "who" the vendor corporation is but also "who" the corporation's representative is. The vendor and the vendor's representative are both inextricably and inevitably part of "the product" that the prospect must judge before he buys. The less tangible the generic product, the more powerfully and persistently the judgment about it is shaped by the "packaging"—how it's presented, who presents it, what's implied by metaphor, simile, symbol, and other surrogates for reality.

So too with tangible products. They do not stand alone on their generic essence. The sales engineers assigned to work with an electric utility company that will ask for competitive bids on a $100-million steam boiler system for its new plant are as powerfully a part of the offered product (the "promise") as the investment banking firm's partner.

The reason is easy to see. In neither case is there a product until it's delivered. You don't know how well it works until it's put and kept at work.

In both investment banking and big boilers, to become the designated vendor requires successful passage through several successive gates, the stages in the sales process. It is not unlike courtship. Both customers know that a rocky courtship spells trouble ahead. If the suitor is not sufficiently solicitous during courtship, if he's insensitive to moods and needs, unresponsive or wavering during stress or adversity, there will be problems in the marriage. But unlike a real marriage, there can be no divorce. Once the deal is made, marriage and gestation have simultaneously begun. After that things are often irreversible. In investment banking, it may take months of close work with the client's organization before the underwriting can be launched, before the baby is born. In the construction of an electric power plant it takes years, through sickness and health. But as with babies, birth presents new problems. All babies must be carefully coddled to see them through early life. Relapse is to be avoided or quickly corrected if it happens. Stocks or bonds should not go quickly to deep discounts. The boiler should not suddenly malfunction after several weeks or months; if it does, it should be rapidly restored to full use. Understandably, the client will, in courtship, note everything carefully, judging always what kind of husband and father the eager suitor is likely to make.

In that sense, the way the product is packaged (how the promise is depicted in brochure, letter, design appearance) and how it is presented and by whom all become parts of the product itself, because they are elements of what it is that the customer finally decides to buy or reject.

A product is more than a tangible thing, even a huge thing like a $100-million boiler. From the buyer's viewpoint, the product is a promise, a cluster of value expectations of which its nontangible parts are as integral as its tangible parts. Certain conditions must be satisfied before the prospect buys. If they are not satisfied, there is no sale. There would have been no sale in the cases of the investment banker and the boiler manufacturer if their representatives had been improperly responsive or insufficiently informed about the customers' special situations and problems during the prebidding (courtship) stages of the relationship. The reason there would have been no sale is that in each case the promised product—the whole product—was not satisfactory. It is not that it was incomplete; it was not right. Changing the "salesman" in midstream is not likely to have helped. In each case the selling organization by then would already have "said" the wrong thing about itself, its product. If, during the courtship, the prospective customer got the impression that there might be aftermarket problems in execution, in timeliness, in the postsale support necessary for smooth and congenial relations, then the customer got a perfectly complete message of what the product would be. It would be bad.

What makes intangible products unique is that they are entirely nonexistent before being bought, entirely incapable of prior inspection or review. For that reason, the customer is forced to make judgments far more on the basis of what's asserted or implied about the product than with tangible products. Assertions and implications must therefore be more carefully managed than with tangible products. Still, in some cases the distinction between the marketing needs of tangible and those of intangible products is negligible. Tangible products that may require considerable or continuing after-sale buyer–seller interaction, or ones that perform functions vital to the continuing effectiveness of the buyer's company (such as, for example, a data processing installation), depend heavily for sales success on assertions and implications made in advance. That is particularly so when tangible products require considerable maintenance help, parts availability, postpurchase adjusting, and application support.

What therefore becomes crucial for sales success is how competitors differentiate themselves from each other. Competing firms offering tangible products differentiate each other by design, operating features, and special-purpose applications. Competing intangible products do so more commonly by surrogates. While similarities abound, the differences are crucial. When offering minicomputers for the international departments of commercial banks, Digital Equipment Corporation (DEC) emphasizes a software package oriented to what it believes are the special needs of those departments. Its major competitors emphasize software oriented to the bank's total information processing and cash management needs. Digital believes that the department, operating as a profit center, is more attracted to a product that *it* can "control" for getting its customer-serving jobs done than to a product (which includes software) that might be preferred by the bank's central data center, whose main concern is record-keeping, or the bank's corporate managers, whose main concern is bankwide cash management. DEC has therefore shifted the battle for competitive advantage not simply away from the capabilities of the computer itself but more significantly to the institutional incentives of its specific users in

100

the customer organization. It has positioned itself in a different competitive quadrant—asserting and implying superior capability of meeting the needs of the users rather than simply of the "corporation" (the bank) that will sign the check. DEC tangibilizes its distinction with software, brochures, and other indicative evidence of its special understanding of and responsiveness to the needs and practices of the bank departments on which it calls.

So much, briefly, for making a sale, for getting a customer. Keeping a customer is quite another thing, and on that score intangible products have very special problems.

Intangible products are by nature highly people-intensive in their production and delivery. Corporate financial services of banks are, in this respect, not so different from hairdressing or consultancy. The more people-intensive a product, the more room there is for personal discretion, idiosyncrasy, error, and delay. Once a customer for an intangible product is sold, the customer can be easily unsold as a consequence of his expectations having been underfulfilled. A tangible product, being manufactured under close supervision in a factory and generally delivered through a planned network of orderly transmission, is much more likely than an intangible product to fulfill the promised expectation. Consider the contrast:

"Goods are produced, services are performed," wrote John M. Rathwell.[1] A tangible product is designed, generally, by design professionals working under conditions of benign isolation, having received guidance from market intelligence experts, scientists, and others. The product will be manufactured by another group of specialists in a facility and with equipment specifically designed for that purpose, generally under conditions of close supervision that facilitate relatively reliable quality control. Installation and use by the customer is guided within a relatively narrow range of possibilities dictated by the product itself.

Intangible products present an entirely different picture.

[1] John M. Rathwell, *Marketing in the Service Sector* (Cambridge, Mass.: Winthrop Publishers, 1974), p. 58.

The computer software designer must do his own research on the customer's premises, trying to understand complex networks of interconnecting operations. Then he designs the system and the software. Having designed it, he has manufactured it. Unlike tangible products, for intangible products design and manufacturing is simultaneous and generally done by the same people. Often they are done by one person alone, like a craftsman at a workbench. Moreover, manufacturing the product is generally indistinguishable from its actual delivery. In situations such as consultancy, from the client's viewpoint, the delivery *is* the manufacturing. If the delivery is an oral presentation that's intended to effect change (as is often the case in consultancy and other expert advisory work), though the study may have been excellent, if the delivery is poor, it will be viewed as having been badly "manufactured." It's a faulty product. So too with the work of brokers of all kinds, restaurants to a considerable extent, educators and trainers, accounting firms, engineering firms, architects, orthodontists, transportation companies, hospitals and clinics, government agencies, banks, trust companies, mutual funds, car rental companies, insurance companies, repair and maintenance operations, and on and on. For each, delivery and production are virtually indistinguishable.

Because these are highly people-intensive operations, there is an enormous problem of quality control. Quality control on an automobile assembly line is in some respects automatic, built into the system. If a yellow door is hung on a red car, somebody on the line will quickly ask if that's what was intended. If the left front wheel is missing, the person next in line, especially if the task is to fasten the lug bolts, will stop the line. But if a commercial banker misses an important feature of a financing package or doesn't do it well, his lapse may never be found or may be found too late. If the ashtrays aren't cleaned on a rented car, discovery is provocative, not preventive: It will annoy or irritate the already committed customer. Repeat business is jeopardized.

No matter how well trained or motivated, people make mistakes, forget, commit indiscretions, at times get hard to handle. Hence the search for alternatives to dependence on people. Automatic telephone switching is not simply cheaper than manual switching, it is far more reliable. Chapter 3 suggests a variety of ways to reduce people dependence in the so-called service industries via what I have called "the industrialization of service." This means substituting "hard," "soft," or "hybrid" technologies for totally people-intensive activities. Examples of a "hard" technology, as noted before, are automatic direct dialing to replace operator-assisted telephone dialing, credit cards replacing repetitive credit checking, and continuous computerized monitoring rather than batch testing of industrial processes. A "soft" technology is the substitution of division of labor for one-person craftsmanship in production—as, for example, organizing the work force that cleans an office building so that each worker specializes in one or several limited tasks (dusting, waxing, vacuuming, window cleaning) rather than have each person do all these jobs alone. Insurance companies long ago went to extensive division of labor in their applications processing—registering, underwriting, actuarying, policy issuing. "Hybrid" technologies combine the soft and the hard. The floor is waxed by machine rather than by hand. French fries are precut and portion-packed in a factory for finishing in a fast-food restaurant in specially designed deep fryers that signal when the process is completed. A computer automatically calculates and makes all entries in an Internal Revenue Service form 1040 after a relatively modestly trained clerk has entered the raw data on a console.

Industrializing systems help control quality and cut costs. To get those results it is important to see what's involved. Instead of depending on people to work better, industrialization redesigns the work so that people work differently. Thus there is applied to service (the production, creation, and delivery of largely intangible products) the same modes of managerial rationality that were first applied to goods production in the nineteenth century. As described more fully in Chapter 9, the real significance of the nineteenth century is not the Industrial Revolution, with its shift from animal to machine power, but the managerial revolution, with its shift from the craftsman's functional independence to the manager's rational routines. In successive waves, the mechanical harvester, the sewing machine, and then the automobile epitomized the genius of the century. Each was rationally designed so as to become an assembled rather than a constructed machine, a machine that depended not on the idiosyncratic artistry of a single craftsman but on simple standardized tasks performed to simple routine specifications by unskilled workers. This required detailed planning and enormous managerial enterprise so that interchangeable parts would be properly designed, manufactured, ordered, and arranged via lifts and jigs for assembly on moving conveyors, and so that large numbers of people would be at the right places at the right times to do the right simple jobs in the right ways. Then, with massive output, distribution and aftermarket training and service systems had to be created and kept going so that the massive output would itself be justified.

What's been largely missing in nontangible goods production is the kind of managerial rationality that produced the Industrial Revolution. That is why the quality of nontangible goods tends to be less reliable than it might be, the costs higher than they should be, and customer satisfaction lower than it need be.

While I have referred to the enormous progress that has in recent years been made on these matters and suggested ways to make still more, there is one characteristic of intangible products that requires special attention for holding customers. Unique to intangible products is that the customer is seldom aware when he's being served well. This is especially so in the case of intangible products that, for the duration of the contract, are consumed almost constantly, such as certain banking services, cleaning services, freight hauling, energy management, maintenance services, telephones, and the like.

Consider an international banking relationship, an insurance relationship, an industrial cleaning relationship. If all goes well, the customer is virtually oblivious to what he's getting. Only when things don't go well or a competitor suggests they could go better does the customer become aware of the product's existence or nonexistence: when a letter of credit is incorrectly drawn; when a competing bank proposes better arrangements; when the annual insurance premium notice arrives or a claim is disputed; when the ashtrays aren't cleaned or a favorite pen holder is missing after the cleaning crew has left.

The most important thing to know about intangible products is that the *customer usually doesn't know what he's getting until he doesn't*. Only when he doesn't get what he bargained for does he become aware of *what* he bargained for. Only on dissatisfaction does he dwell. Satisfaction is, as it should be, mute. Its prior presence is affirmed only by its subsequent absence.

And that's dangerous, because the customer will be aware only of failure, of dissatisfaction, not of success or satisfaction. That makes him terribly susceptible to the blandishments of competitive sellers. A competitor can always structure a more interesting corporate financing deal, can always propose a more imaginative insurance program, can always find dust on top of the picture frame in the office, can always cite small visible failures that imply big hidden ones and vendor neglect.

Thus, while in *getting* customers for intangibles it becomes important to create surrogates or metaphors for tangibility— how we dress, how we speak, write, design and present proposals, work with prospects, respond to inquiries, initiate ideas, show how well we understand the prospect's business—in *keeping* customers for intangibles it becomes important regularly to remind the customers of what they're regularly getting. If that's not done, the customer will not know. He'll only know when he's *not* getting what he bought, and that's all that's likely to count unless, in the interval, he's been made so regularly and persuasively aware of what he's been getting all along that occasional failures fade in relative importance.

To keep customers for regularly delivered and consumed intangible products, they have to be regularly reminded of what they're getting. The promises that were made in order to land the customer must be regularly reinstated when the promises are fulfilled. Even the source of the delivered product has to be regularly reinstated in the customer's consciousness lest he forget who his anonymous and silent vendor is.

When an insurance prospect is heavily romanced and finally accepts marriage, the subsequent silence and inattention can be deafening. Most customers seldom recall for long what kind of life insurance package they bought, often forgetting as well the name of both underwriter and agent. To be reminded a year later via a premium notice reminds one only of the disjunction between the loving attention in courtship and the long cold silence in marriage. No wonder the lapse rate in personal life insurance is so high.

Once a relationship is cemented, equity is created for the seller. He has a customer. To help keep him, the equity in that relationship must be enhanced lest it decline and become jeopardized by competitors.

There are innumerable ways to do that, and some of these can be industrialized. Periodic letters or phone calls that remind the customer of how well things are going are low-cost and surprisingly powerful equity maintainers. Newsletters or regular visits suggesting new or better or augmented product features are useful. Even nonbusiness socializing has its value, as is acknowledged and affirmed by corporations struggling in recent years with the Internal Revenue Service about the deductability of hunting lodges, yachts, clubs, and spouses attending conferences and customer meetings at exotic watering holes in distant places.

Here are some examples of how companies have strengthened their relationships with customers:

—An energy management company sends out a periodic "Update Report" on conspicuous yellow paper, advising clients how to discover and correct energy leaks, install improved monitors, and accomplish cost savings.
—A computer service bureau organizes its account managers for a two-week series of blitz customer callbacks to "explain casually" the installation of new central processing equipment that is expected to prevent cost increases next year while expanding the customers' interactive options.
—A long-distance hauler of high-value electronic equip-

ment (computers, terminals, mail sorters, word processors, medical diagnostic instruments) has instituted quarterly performance reviews with its shippers, some of which include customers who are encouraged to talk about their experiences and expectations.

—An insurance company sends periodic one-page notices to policyholders *and* policy beneficiaries. These generally begin with a single-sentence congratulation that policy and coverage remain nicely intact and follow with brief views on recent tax rulings affecting insurance, new notions about personal financial planning, and special protection packages available with other types of insurance.

In all these ways, sellers of intangible products reinstate their presence and performance in the customers' minds, reminding them of their continuing presence and the value of what is constantly, and silently, being delivered.

All products have elements of tangibility and intangibility. Companies that sell tangible products invariably promise more than the tangible products themselves. Indeed, enormous dedication, often in pretentious proportions, focuses on the enhancement of the intangibles—promises about bountiful benefits conferred rather than on features offered. To the buyer of photographic film, Kodak promises with unremitting emphasis just one thing, the satisfactions of enduring remembrance, memories clearly preserved. Wisely, Kodak says almost nothing about the superior luminescence of its pictures. The product is remembrance, not film or pictures. The promoted product of the automobile, as everyone knows, is certainly not transportation. Auto companies promote what people respond to most in their minds, not what the manufacturers make most effectively in their factories. Auto dealers, on the other hand, assuming correctly that people's minds have already been reached by the manufacturers' ads, focus on other considerations: deals, availability, postpurchase servicing. Neither the dealers nor the manufacturers "sell" the tangible cars themselves. They "sell" the intangible benefits that are bundled into the entire package: the total product, with considerable emphasis these days on fuel efficiency.

If tangible products must be intangibilized to add customer-getting appeal, then intangible products must be tangibilized—what Professor Leonard L. Berry calls "managing the evidence."[2] Ideally, this should be done as a matter of routine without the necessity of intervening personal promises or reassurances. It should be industrialized. Hotels do this regularly. In their bathrooms the drinking glasses are wrapped in fresh bags or film, the toilet seat has a "sanitized" paper band, the end piece of the toilet tissue is neatly shaped into a fresh-looking arrowhead. All these say with silent affirmative clarity that "the room has been specially cleaned for your use and comfort," yet no words are spoken to say it. Words, in any case, would be less convincing, nor could employees be reliably depended on to say them each time or say them convincingly. Hotels thus have not only tangibilized their promise but also industrialized its delivery. It's become a nonpersonalized routine.

Take, on the other hand, the instructive case of house insulation, a necessity most homeowners approach with understandable apprehension. Suppose you call two companies to bid on your house. The first insulation installer arrives in his car. After pacing once around the house with measured self-assurance and making quick calculations on back of an envelope, he confidently quotes $2,400 for six-inch fiberglass, total satisfaction guaranteed. Another drives up in a clean white truck with clipboard in hand. He scrupulously measures the house dimensions, counts the windows, crawls the attic, records from a source book the area's seasonal temperature ranges and wind velocities. He asks a host of questions, meanwhile recording everything with obvious diligence. He then promises to return in three days, which he does, with a typed proposal for six-inch fiberglass insulation at $2,600, total satisfaction guaranteed. From which will you buy?

The latter has tangibilized the intangible, made a promise

---

[2] Leonard L. Berry, "Service Marketing Is Different," *Business,* May–June 1980, pp. 24–29.

into a credible expectation. Even more persuasive tangibility is provided by an insulation firm whose representative types the relevant information into a portable intelligent printing terminal. The analysis and response are almost instant, causing one user to call it "the most powerful tool ever developed in the insulation industry." If the house owner is head of the project buying team of an electric utility company, the treasurer of a mighty corporation, the materials purchasing agent of a ready-mixed cement company, the transportation manager of a fertilizer manufacturer, or the data processing director of an insurance company, it's almost certain he will make vendor decisions in his work the same way as he did for his house. He requires the risk-reducing reassurance of tangibilized intangibles.

The practice of providing reassuring tangibilizations of the intangible—of the promise—can be effectively employed even when the generic product is itself tangible. Laundry detergents that claim special whitening capabilities make the promise credible with "blue whitener beads" that are clearly visible to the user. Proctor & Gamble's new decaffeinated instant coffee (High Point) attests to coffee genuineness with luminescent "milled flakes for hearty, robust flavor." You can *see* what the claims promise.

Getting customers for an intangible product requires the product to be tangibilized. Keeping customers for an intangible product requires the product to be reinstated, to be constantly resold while things go well lest the customer get lost when things go badly. Doing both well requires that the tasks be industrialized. The relationship with the customer has to be managed much more carefully and continuously in the case of intangible than tangible products, though it is vital in both cases. Managing the relationship is in itself another topic. It rises in importance as products become more complex and links between buyer and seller are required by the necessity of that complexity to become more intimate and stretch out over greater periods of time, often much longer than any of the parties to the transactions remain in their jobs. "Relationship management" is a special important subject all its own. It is treated separately in Chapter 6.

Meanwhile, the importance of what I've tried to say here is

emphasized by one overriding fact: A customer is an asset that's usually more precious than the tangible assets on the balance sheet. You can usually buy balance sheet assets. There are lots of willing sellers. You cannot so easily buy customers. They are far less willing than are sellers and have lots of eager sellers offering them many choices. Moreover, a customer is a double asset: First, he is the direct source of cash from the sale, and second, his existence can be used to raise cash from bankers and investors, cash that can be converted into tangible assets.

The old chestnut that "Nothing happens till you make a sale," is awfully close to an important truth. What it increasingly takes to make and keep that sale is to tangibilize the intangible, to restate the benefit and its source to the customer, and to industrialize the processes that are involved in doing these.

6

Relationship Management

The relationship between a seller and a buyer seldom ends when the sale is made. In a great and increasing proportion of transactions, the relationship actually intensifies subsequent to the sale. This becomes the critical factor in the buyer's choice of the seller the next time around. This is certainly true of all financial services, consultancy, general contracting, the military and space equipment industries, capital goods, and any vendor organization involving a continuous stream of transactions between seller and buyer.

The sale merely consummates the courtship. Then the marriage begins. How good the marriage is depends on how well the relationship is managed by the seller. That determines whether there will be continued or expanded business or troubles and divorce, and whether costs or profits increase.

In some cases divorce is impossible, as when a major construction or installation project is under way. What remains is a

111

burdened and costly marriage that tarnishes the seller's reputation. Companies can avoid troubles and enhance their standing by recognizing at the outset the necessity of managing their relationship with customers.

This takes more than what comes normally in good marketing. It takes special attention geared to what uniquely characterizes a relationship. That is *time*. The economic theory of "supply and demand" is totally false in this respect. It presumes that the work of the economic system is time discrete and absent of human interactions—an instantaneous, disembodied sales transaction clears the market at the intersection of supply and demand. This was never so and is increasingly less so as growing product complexity and interdependencies among the institutions of the industrial system intensify. The buyer of automated machinery does not, like the buyer at a flea market, walk home with his purchase and take his chances. He expects installation services, applications aids, parts, postpurchase repair and maintenance, retrofitted enhancements, and vendor R & D in support of the buyer's need to stay competitive in all respects. The buyer of a continuous stream of transactions, like a frozen food manufacturer who buys cartons from a packaging company and cash-management services from a bank, is concerned not with "clearing the market" but rather with maintaining the process. With the growing complexity of military equipment, it is not surprising that 78 percent of the U.S. defense budget now goes for items in units of less than a hundred. Growing complexity and increasing costs lead to a growing need for continuous services and enhancements in order to keep the product longer in effective and state-of-the-art use.

The purchase cycles of products and major components gets increasingly stretched, and this changes the nature of what needs to be attended to. Consider the purchase cycles of the following:

Oil field installations	15–20 years
Chemical plant	10–15 years
EDP system	5–10 years

Weapons system	20–30 years
Steel plant major components	5–10 years
Paper supply contract	5 years

And consider the changing character of assurances under which purchases are being made:

LONG-TERM ASSURANCES

Subject	From	→	To
Tankers	Spot		Charter
Apartments	Rental		Cooperative
Auto warrants	10,000		50,000
Technology	Buy		Lease
Labor	Hire		Contracts
Supplies	Shopping		Contracting
Equipment	Repair		Maintenance

In these conditions a purchase decision is not a decision to buy an item (to have, as in modern life, an affair), but a decision to enter a bonded relationship (to have a marriage). This requires of the would-be seller a new orientation and a new strategy. Marketing by itself is no longer enough. Consider the compelling differences between the old and the new. Consider selling:

Sales Department

Here the seller, living at a distance from the buyer, reaches out with his sales department to unload onto the buyer what the seller has decided to make. This is the basis for the notion that a salesman needs charisma, because it is charisma that makes the sale rather than the product selling itself. Consider, by contrast, marketing:

113

Here the seller, living closer to the buyer, penetrates the buyer's domain to learn about his needs, desires, fears, and the like, and then designs and supplies the product in all its forms. Instead of trying to get the buyer to want what the seller has, the seller tries to have what the buyer will want. The "product" is no longer merely an item but a whole bundle of value satisfactions —what in Chapter 4 I called the "augmented product."

With increasing interdependence, more and more of the world's economic work gets done through long-term relationships between sellers and buyers. It is not just that once you get a customer you want to keep him. It is more a matter of what the buyer wants. He wants a vendor who keeps his promises, who'll keep supplying and stand behind what he promised. The age of the blind date or the one-night stand is gone. Marriage is both more convenient and more necessary. Products are too complicated, repeat negotiations too much of a hassle and too costly. In these conditions success in marketing, like success in marriage, is transformed into the inescapability of a relationship. The interface is transformed into interdependence.

To be, under these circumstances, a good marketer in the conventional sense is not good enough. When it takes five years of intensive, close work between seller and buyer during which the previous signing of a contract is converted into the "delivery" of, say, an operating chemical plant or a telecommunications system, more will have to be done than in the kind of marketing that landed the contract at the outset. The buyer needs assurance at the outset that the two parties will live congenially together during the long period in which the purchase is transformed into delivery.

The seller and the buyer have different capital structures, face different competitive conditions and costs, and have different incentive structures and different purposes respecting the commitments they have made to each other. The seller has made a sale, which he expects directly to yield a profit. The buyer has bought a tool with which to produce things to yield a profit. *For the seller it is the end of the process; for the buyer the beginning.* Yet their interdependence is inextricable, inescapable, and profound. To make the dependencies of these totally different and differently motivated entities work and to keep them trouble-free requires that the relationships be understood and that their management be planned for in advance of the marriage itself. To get out the marriage manual after trouble has begun is to have done so too late.

The future will be a future of more and more intensified relationships, especially in industrial marketing, but also increasingly even in frequently purchased consumer goods. Thus Procter & Gamble, copying General Mills' Betty Crocker advisory service, has found that the installation of a consumer hotline to give advice on its products and their uses raised customer brand loyalty.

The future is best understood with reference to the past and the present. These may be best seen with respect to specific matters in industrial settings, as set forth in the accompanying table (p. 116).

The defining characteristic of the terms in the column on "Future" is time. What is labeled "Item" in the first row was, in the past, simply a product, something that was bought for its own value. More recently that simple product was not enough. What was bought was an "augmented product." In the era we are entering more will be required. It will be system contracts, characterized by a complex congeries of continuous contacts and evolving relationships that surround the systems. The "Sale" will be a system over time, not just a system itself. The

115

Category	Past	Present	Future
Item	Product	Augmented product	System contracts
Sale	Unit	System	System/time
Value	Feature advantage	Technology advantages	System advantages
Lead time	Short	Long	Lengthy
Service	Modest	Important	Vital
Delivery place	Local	National	Global
Delivery phase	Once	Frequently	Continuous
Strategy	Sales	Marketing	Relationship

"Value" that is at stake will pertain to the advantages of that total system over time. As the customer gains more experience with it over time, the technology will decline in importance relative to the system of benefits in which the technology is embedded. More important than technology will be the other benefits and interactions, like services, delivery, reliability, responsiveness, and the quality of the human and organizational interactions between seller and buyer over time.

The management of industrial marketing contracts deals with coexistence and communications over time. The object is to fulfill the customer's expectations so as to earn his loyalty and thus his continued patronage, preferably at a level of satisfaction that will be reflected in above-average margins.

The more complex the system, and the more "software" it requires (such as its operating procedures and protocols, its management routines, its service components), and the longer it takes to implement the system, the greater the customer's anxieties and expectations. *Expectations* are what people buy, not things. They buy the expectations of benefits promised by the vendor. When it takes a long time to fulfill the promise (such as the delivery of a new custom-made automated work station), or if fulfillment is continuous over a long period (such as banking services, fuel to run your facilities, or components for your assembly operations), the buyer's anxieties build up after the purchase decision is made. Will the delivery be prompt? Will it be smooth and regular? Did we select the best vendor?

When downstream realities loom larger than up-front promises, what do you do before, during, and after the sale? Who will be responsible for what?

To answer these questions it helps to understand how the customer's expectations are shaped by the promises and behavior of the vendor before the sale is made. If you promise the moon, it is reasonable for the customer to expect it. If those who do the selling and the marketing, however, operate on commissions paid out before the customer gets everything he bargained for, or if they sell against high quotas, they're not likely to feel any strong compulsion to assure that the moon actually gets fully and reliably delivered. After the sale they'll rush off to pursue other prey. If marketing plans the sale, sales make it, manufacturing fulfills it, and service services it, who's in charge and who feels responsible?

Problems arise not only because those who do the selling, the marketing, the manufacturing, and the servicing have different incentives and, as a result, view the customer differently, but also because organizations are themselves one-dimensional. An organization necessarily internalizes itself, even though it may depend on externals (customers) for its fate. "Inside" is where the work gets done, where the workplace is, where the penalties and incentives reside, where the budgets and plans are made, where engineering and manufacturing take place, where performance is measured, where one's friends and associates are, where things are managed and manageable and the outside is where "you can't change things," and besides, it "has nothing to do with me." Those for whom the outside clearly "has something to do with me" are the people in sales and marketing. But there are lots of disjunctions between seller and buyer regarding the object of the sale, and these differ at different stages of the sale. These may be simply stated (Table A, p. 118). When the first sale is finally made, different things happen to the seller and to the buyer. These create the basis for a lot of dissonance (Table B, p. 118).

The fact of buying changes the buyer. He expects the seller to remember the purchase as having been a favor bestowed on him by the buyer, not as something earned by the seller. Hence

117

A. STAGES AND OBJECTS OF THE SALE

Stage of Sale	Seller	Buyer
1. Before	Real hope	Vague need
2. Romance	Hot & heavy	Testing & hopeful
3. Sale	Fantasy—bed	Fantasy—board
4. After	Looks elsewhere for next sale	"You don't care."
5. Long after	Indifferent	"Can't this be made better?"
6. Next sale	"How about a new one?"	"Really?"

B. WHEN THE FIRST SALE IS MADE

The Seller	The Buyer
Objective achieved	Judgment postponed, applies test of time
Selling stops	Shopping continues
Focus goes elsewhere	Focus on purchase, wants affirmation of expectations
Tension released	Tension increased
Relationship reduced or ended	Relationship intensified, commitment made

it is wrong to assume that to have gained an account gives you an advantage by virtue of having gotten "a foot in the door." The opposite is increasingly the case. If the buyer views the sale as a favor conferred by him on the seller, then he in effect debits the seller's account. The seller owes him one. The seller is in the position of having to rebuild his relationship from a deficit position.

In the absence of good management, the relationship deteriorates because of the differences between the buyer and the seller in their needs, wants, and incentive structures and because both organizations tend naturally to face inward to their internal affairs rather than outward toward each other. Inward orientation by the selling organization leads to insensitivity and unresponsiveness in customer relations, at best to the substitution of bureaucratic formalities for authentic interactions. Thus the things that build bad relationships accumulate while good ones suffer.

The natural tendency of relationships, whether in marriage

or in business, is entropy—the erosion or deterioration of sensitivity and attentiveness. A healthy relationship maintains, and preferably expands, the equity and the possibilities that were created during courtship. A healthy relationship requires a conscious and constant fight against the forces of entropy. It becomes important for the seller regularly and seriously to ask himself, for example, "How are we doing?" "Is the relationship improving or deteriorating?" "Are our promises being fully fulfilled?" "Are we neglecting anything?" "How do we stand vis-à-vis our competitors in the relationship?" Consider the good things that might be done and the bad things that are done to affect relationships with buyers (Table C).

C. THINGS AFFECTING RELATIONSHIPS

Good Things	Bad Things
Initiate positive phone calls	Make only callbacks
Make recommendations	Make justifications
Candor in language	Accommodative language
Use phone	Use correspondence
Show appreciation	Wait for misunderstandings
Make service suggestions	Wait for service requests
Use "we" problem-solving language	Use "owe-us" legal language
Get to problems	Only respond to problems
Use jargon/shorthand	Use long-winded communications
Personality problems aired	Personality problems hidden
Talk of "our future together"	Talk about making good on the past
Routinize responses	Fire drill/emergency responsiveness
Accept responsibility	Shift blame
Plan the future	Rehash the past

One of the surest signs of a bad or declining relationship is the absence of complaints from the customer. Nobody is ever *that* satisfied, especially not over an extended period of time. The customer is either not being candid or not being contacted. Probably both. Communication is impaired. The absence of candor reflects the decline of trust, the deterioration of the relationship. Bad things accumulate. The relationship depreciates. As in marriage, impaired communication is both a symptom and a cause of trouble. Things fester inside. When they finally erupt, it's usually too late, or very costly.

119

Your next sale, next product, next idea, next success depend a lot on your external relationships. A good relationship is an asset. We can invest in relationships and we can borrow from them. We all do it, but we seldom account for it and almost never manage it. Yet a company's most precious asset is its relationships with its customers. It is not "who you know" but how you are known to them. And that is a function of the nature of your relationships with them, which depends on how they have been managed.

Not all relationships can be or need to be at the same level of intimacy or of the same duration. These characteristics depend on the extent of the actual or felt dependencies between the buyers and the sellers. And, of course, those dependencies can be extended or contracted by means of various direct links that can be established between buyer and seller. Thus, when Bergen Burnswig, the booming drug and health care products distributor, puts computer terminals in its customers' offices to enable them to order directly and get instant feedback regarding their shelf movement, inventory, and other valuable information, a new dependency link has been created that helps tie the customer to the vendor. At the same time, however, there are important ways in which the seller becomes dependent on the buyer. The most obvious resides in the buyer's ability to withdraw his custom or reduce the percentage of buying he does with that vendor. Less obvious is that the buyer is, or can be, an important source of important information for the seller. How much is the buyer's own business likely to change, and therefore how will he buy in the future? What are the substitute products or materials, and what variety of prices and services is being offered to the buyer by competitors who seek his business and the business of other customers or potential customers? How well are we fulfilling the customer's needs and expectations? Is our performance in the field up to our promises from headquarters? To what new uses is the customer putting our product, or how is he using it differently?

The accuracy of forecasts regarding the buyer's intentions rests on the quality of the relationship with him. In a good relationship the buyer shares his plans and expectations with the vendor or at least makes it possible to know his intentions. Surprises and bad forecasts are symptoms of bad relationships. Everybody loses, even the buyer. With better information the vendor can better serve and therefore better hold the buyer. Everybody benefits.

Thus there is a system of reciprocal dependencies. It is up to the seller to develop the relationship beyond that supposed by the simple notion of keeping a customer merely for the contribution he makes to the seller's current revenues and profits. In a proper relationship both the buyer and the seller should have a "profit." Otherwise the relationship cannot last. Moreover, acquisition costs are rarely the only costs of what's being bought. Postpurchase costs are almost always inevitable. Somebody has to bear or share them. This means that the vendor should work at getting his customer to want to maintain the vendor's long-term profitability at an acceptable level instead of squeezing to get rock-bottom delivered prices. Nor is the low-cost producer necessarily the low-cost supplier, even when his price reflects his costs. Unless the costs of the expected postpurchase services are also somehow reflected in the price, the buyer will end up paying more—in money, in delays, and in aggravation. That is no way to build and maintain a healthy relationship, no way to keep a customer. The smart relationship manager on the vendor side will help the buyer to do long-term life-cycle costing in assessing the vendor's offering.

It is not surprising that in professional partnerships, such as law, medicine, architecture, consulting, investment banking, and advertising, individuals are rated and rewarded by the client relationships they control. Those relationships, like any other assets, can appreciate or depreciate. Their maintenance and enhancement are not a matter of good manners, public relations, tact, charm, window dressing, or manipulation. They have to do with management, and not just marketing, because it transcends what marketing uniquely does. Relationship management requires companywide programs for maintenance, investment, improvement, and also for replacement. The results can be spectacular.

Consider the case of the North Sea oil and gas fields. Norway and Britain did a great deal to urge and facilitate exploration and development. They were eager and even generous hosts to the oil companies that spent hundreds of millions to do their work. Suddenly, when oil and gas started flowing, the host countries levied taxes running to more than 90 percent of the market prices. Nobody was more surprised than the companies. Why surprised? Would having built sound relationships with the governments, by whatever means, so as to have created a sense of mutuality and partnership have reduced the size of the taxes? What would it have been worth? Nor is this an isolated situation. It applies in other similar undertakings where the vendor or coventurer is required to make heavy advance expenditures to get the account and develop the product. This is represented by the depiction in Figure 2 of cash flows to such a vendor during the life of the account. As is shown, during the customer-getting and development period, cash flows are negative, with the customer eagerly encouraging the expenditures. When the product is delivered or the joint venture becomes operative, cumulative cash flows turn up and finally become positive. In the case of the North Sea, the surprising new high taxes represent the difference between what revenues to the oil companies might have been (the upper dotted line) and what they became (the solid line). With worse relationships, they might, of course, have fallen to the lower dotted line.

Consider also the case of Gillette North America. It has four separate sales forces. There are special programs for major accounts designed to help them with their businesses and assure the rapid and smooth response of Gillette to the requirements of those businesses. But in addition there is a vice president of business relations who has among his major duties, separate from the sales organization, the cultivation of Gillette's relationships with major retailers and distributors via a vast array of ceremonial activities, ranging from hosting cocktail parties, dinners, and entertainments at twelve trade association conventions annually, to the organization of special events for major accounts in connection with the annual All-Star baseball game, the World Series, the Super Bowl, and the NCAA playoffs, and to attending special events like trade-sponsored charitable din-

FIGURE 2.   CUMULATIVE CASH FLOW HISTORY OF AN ACCOUNT

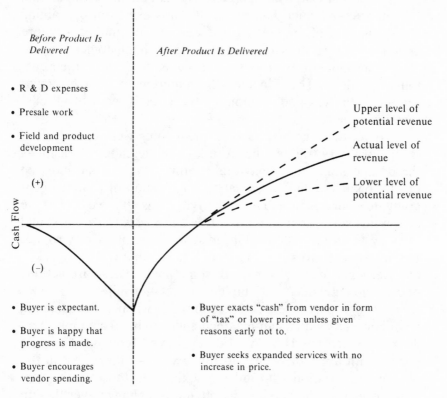

Before Product Is Delivered

After Product Is Delivered

• R & D expenses

• Presale work

• Field and product development

(+)

Cash Flow

(−)

Upper level of potential revenue

Actual level of revenue

Lower level of potential revenue

• Buyer is expectant.

• Buyer is happy that progress is made.

• Buyer encourages vendor spending.

• Buyer exacts "cash" from vendor in form of "tax" or lower prices unless given reasons early not to.

• Buyer seeks expanded services with no increase in price.

ners and retirement parties for presidents of major retail chains. Bonds are built, trust is established, and reciprocal obligations and benefits are implicitly affirmed.

Many companies do much the same. But it is only part of a more genuinely intensive effort. Many companies have specific response-sensitive and personalizing protocols and routines to handle customer inquiries, requests, and complaints. Some companies now require engineering and manufacturing people to spend time with customers and users in the field—not just to look for product and design ideas, not just for feedback regarding present products and for sensitivity enhancement for themselves, but also to get to know and to respond to customers in deeper and more abiding ways, in short, to build relationships and bonds that last. The Sperry Corporation's much advertised "listening" campaign has taken the in-house form of training large numbers of employees to listen and communicate more effectively as regards each other and their customers. Some companies have formal programs designed to enhance their customer relations. These include the requirement to take regular service initiatives and to monitor the effectiveness of all customer relations.

To get these going and keep them going well requires constant sensitivity training, because nothing degrades so easily as the practices and the behavioral routines that are and must be institutionalized. This necessary formalization of routines generally degenerates into faceless activity. It is all too easy to take action instead of spending time. It is all too easy to act first and then try to fix the relationship, instead of the other way round. It is all too easy to say, "We'll look into it and call you back," or "Let's get together for lunch sometime." These are actions of diversion and delay, not builders of relationships.

When a purchase cycle is long—as when a beer-making plant contracts with a can-making vendor to build a factory next door, or when the U.S. Air Force "buys" (commits to) a jet engine with a life of twenty to thirty years—the people in the vendor organization who did the selling and those in the customer organization who did the buying will change over the life of those "contracts." So, in all likelihood, will the entire upper levels of management on both sides. What needs to be done by the seller to assure continuity of good relations? What is expected by the customer when people who did the buying are gone and replaced?

Clearly, relationship management requires not just the care of little things day in and day out but also the cumulative constructive management of all things large and small throughout the organization. The idea is to build bonds that last, no matter who comes and goes.

The management of relationships requires the creation and constant nurturing of systems to manage them, to maintain and enhance them. As in the management of anything, this requires four familiar old steps, shopworn as they may seem.

124

1. *Awareness:* Show that it is a problem, and that the problem has costs. Show that it is an opportunity, and that the opportunity has benefits.
2. *Assessment:* Determine where the company now stands, especially as compared with what's necessary to get the desired results.
3. *Accountability:* Establish regular reporting on individual relationships, and then on group relationships, so that these can be weighed against other measures of performance.
4. *Actions:* Make decisions and allocations, and establish routines and communications on the basis of their impact on the targeted relationships. Constantly reinforce awareness and actions.

Checklists can, of course, be provided to help assure that all the proper things are regularly done. The problem with checklists is that they get to be mindlessly employed, thus becoming ritualized substitutes for thought and substance. Designed to achieve coverage, they require nobody to become deeply sensitized to the substance of the relationships or seriously committed to their purposes. Nobody needs seriously to look, listen, think, or get involved; one needs only to check things antiseptically off.

Relationship management can be institutionalized, but in the process it also has to be humanized. One company has regular sensitivity sessions and role-playing seminars in which members of the vendor firm assume the roles of the buyer. It also conducts in-depth debriefings on meetings with customers. Regularly with its various accounts it requires its customer-contact people (including those who make deliveries and handle receivables) to ask the seminal "relationship" questions: How are we doing in the relationship? Is it going up or down? How much are we talking with them, about what, and with whom? What have we not done lately? The emphasis on "lately" is not exceptional. It recognizes that relationships naturally degrade and have to be reinstated. If I owe you a favor, I forget, but you don't. And when I've done you a favor, you feel obliged, but

125

not for long. You ask, "What have you done for me lately?" A relationship credit must be used, or it vanishes. It must be used soon, or it depreciates.

The institutionalization of relationship management is also possible by establishing routines that assure the right kinds of customer contacts. Consider what was done by a well-known Wall Street investment firm. It required its security analysts and salesmen to make regular constructive contacts with their institutional customers. "Constructive" was defined as conveying useful information to them. Hence the firm developed a regular Monday morning investment strategy "commentary," which analysts and salesmen could convey by telephone to their customers. In addition, each analyst was required to develop periodic industry commentaries and updates, to be either mailed or phoned to customers. Analysts and salesmen were required to keep telephone logs of these contacts, which were collected, compiled, counted, and communicated in a companywide report that was openly distributed to all salesmen and analysts each week, complete with their names and the names of the individuals and companies contacted. Low-contact salesmen and analysts were required to explain their inactions to their supervisors. End-of-year bonuses were determined not only on the basis of commissions earned from the various institutions, but on the basis of the number and types of contacts individuals had with them. Meanwhile, sensitivity training sessions were regularly conducted in order to enhance the nature of the contacts and the quality of the relationships. The results, which turned out to be highly successful, were carefully analyzed and made known to all participants, thus reinforcing their willingness to continue and the care with which they did so.

Relationship management is a special field all its own. It is as important in preserving and enhancing the intangible asset commonly known as "goodwill" as the management of hard assets. The fact that it is probably harder to do is that much more reason that hard effort be expended to do it.

7

The Marketing Imagination

Nothing drives progress like the imagination. The idea precedes the deed. The only exceptions are accidents and natural selection, but these cannot be willed. Ideas can be willed, and the imagination is their engine. Though progress starts with the imagination, only work can make things happen. And work itself works best when fueled, again, by the imagination. An idea or a new conceptualization usually requires the imaginative application of effort to get the intended results. Thus the imagination gets the idea and then, to be effective, must help convert it into results.

The marketing imagination is the starting point of success in marketing. It is distinguished from other forms of imagination by the unique insights it brings to understanding customers, their problems, and the means to capture their attention and their custom. By asserting that people don't buy things but buy solutions to problems, the marketing imagination makes an inspired leap from the obvious to the meaningful. "Meaning" resides in its implied suggestion as to what to do—in this case, find out what problems people are trying to solve. It is represented by Charles Revson's famous distinction regarding the business of Revlon, Inc.: "In the factory we make cosmetics. In the store we sell hope." It is characterized by Leo McGinneva's famous clarification about why people buy quarter-inch drill bits: "They don't want quarter-inch bits. They want quarter-inch holes." It leads to Professor Raymond A. Bauer's famous point that when buyers select a known vendor or known brand over another it is more meaningful to think of the choice as an act of risk reduction rather than as the expression of a brand preference.

Each of these reconceptualizations found a deeper meaning in customer behavior, thus causing marketing programs to be reshaped in ways better to attract and hold customers. To attract a customer, you are asking him to do something different from what he would have done in the absence of the programs you direct at him. He has to change his mind and his actions. The customer must shift his behavior in the direction advocated by the seller. Hence the seller must distinguish himself and his offering from those of others so that people will want, or at least prefer, to do business with him. The search for meaningful distinction is a central part of the marketing effort. If marketing is seminally about anything, it is about achieving customer-getting distinction by differentiating what you do and how you operate. All else is derivative of that and only that.

Differentiation represents an imaginative response to the existence of potential customers in such a way as to give them compelling reasons to want to do business with the originating supplier. To differentiate an offering effectively requires knowing what drives and attracts customers. It requires knowing how customers differ from one another and how those differences can be clustered into commercially meaningful segments.

If you're not thinking segments, you're not thinking. To think segments means you have to think about what drives customers, customer groups, and the choices that are or might be available to them. To think segments means to think beyond what's obviously out there to see. If everybody sees segments as obviously consisting of certain demographics, industries, user groups, buying practices, certain influencing groups, and the like, then the thinking that gives real power is thinking that transcends the ordinary. Consider the following ad:

> Men Wanted for Hazardous Journey. Small
> wages, bitter cold, long months of complete
> darkness, constant danger, safe return doubtful.
> Honor and recognition in case of success.
> —Ernest Shackleton

The ad, written by the famed polar explorer Sir Ernest Shackleton, appeared in London newspapers in 1900. It yielded an immediate response of unprecedented proportions. Its imaginative appeal was clearly to people for whom honor and recognition were, as they say, everything. Its power lay not only in the novel idea of appealing to the human desire for honor and recognition, though the risks were grave and the work terrible, but also in its deadly frankness and remarkably simple execution.

The discovery of the simple essence of things is the essence of the marketing imagination. In 1974 Milton Greenberg, chief executive of the GCA Corporation, set out to expand his company's dollar share of the various pieces of equipment used to make semiconductor devices. None of his several competitors manufactured a full line. Hence, complementary equipment from several capital goods manufacturers stood cheek by jowl in all the world's semiconductor factories, each doing a separate part of the job in the various steps of semiconductor production. To expand its share of that equipment market, GCA might have tried to displace, with superior equipment, the other suppliers whose equipment stood adjacent to its own in the production line. Instead of setting out to do that (say, make faster and cheaper equipment), GCA set out to displace existing equipment with a machine that combined several production steps in one. Its resulting DSW Waferstepper®, though slower than the competing equipment it replaced and more costly by a factor of three, was a spectacular technical and commercial success. By combining several production operations into a single piece of equipment, it reduced the amount of manual handling of the materials being processed, thus reducing contamination and thereby raising yields. By making the equipment more compact laterally but taller, it saved manufacturing floor space. By improving the lens used in the photolithographic process, it narrowed the line widths and thus raised the operating capacities of the semiconductor chips that the DSW helped produce.

Thus through a single major simplifying R&D effort that was designed to displace rather than merely improve existing equipment, it swept the DSW Waferstepper® suddenly to market dominance. That effort was based on a notion about what the market would really value. Higher yields, more capacity per chip, and better use of factory floor space became the target and the result.

Industry watchers hailed it as a prodigious technological achievement. GCA doesn't deny that. But in its corporate corridors people speak about it mostly as a great marketing achievement—not simply having done things well technologically, but having known what to do. The "what" was the result of the marketing imagination.

Imagination means to construct mental pictures of what is or is not actually present, what has never been actually experienced. To exercise the imagination is to be creative. It requires intellectual or artistic inventiveness. Anybody can do it, and most people often do—unfortunately, however, only in daydreams and fantasies, when they're not constrained by convention or conviction. To do it in business requires shedding these constraints but also discipline, especially the discipline of dissociation from what exists and what has been. It usually requires combining disparate facts or ideas into new amalgamations of meanings.

In marketing, as I have said, the object is to get and keep a customer, and also to get existing buyers to prefer to do business with you rather than your competitors. In marketing, therefore, the imagination must constantly focus on that objective.

Consider the following example from DuPont. Over the years the price for one of its materials used by medical supply manufacturers gradually fell, as did the prices of competitors producing the chemically identical materials. In plotting those prices, it was discovered that DuPont continued over those years to get a slight premium over its competitors, though the premium gap tended to narrow as the years went on. DuPont's market share remained stable. In-depth interviews with customers' design engineers, purchasing people, and manufacturing heads gradually led the DuPont investigators to the conclusion that DuPont's materials, though chemically identical to all others, were believed to be in some way purer and and that DuPont was more likely than others to come out with materials improvements. That, it was concluded, accounted for DuPont's premium.

The discovery of all this was, actually, quite imaginative. What was done with it was dramatically imaginative. DuPont created a series of trade journal advertisements and trade show demonstrations that showed how it took special care to assure the purity of its delivered products. The ads showed a series of quality assurance checks, which DuPont regularly made in the manufacturing process, using electron spectroscophy to test purity at various production stages. At trade shows electron spectroscophy test displays were erected for actual use by those attending the shows for testing batches of materials taken from various stages of the manufacturing process.

Remarkably, over the succeeding years DuPont's narrowing price premiums began to widen, and its market share rose. Follow-up trade research indicated that DuPont's reputation for product purity had risen. The marketing imagination had obviously worked.

Or consider American Express. Its green credit card ("Don't leave home without it," itself an imaginative positioning with great power) is also sold as a "Corporate Card." Corporations have been persuaded to issue it to certain classes of employees instead of giving them cash advances. This helps companies conserve cash and more closely monitor expenses. In 1982 American Express shifted the Corporate Card operations into its Travel Services Division. The Travel Services Division operated, among some other things, travel agencies, making airline and hotel reservations and procuring tickets.

Travel Services concluded that the larger and more geographically dispersed a corporation, the greater was the variety of its travel arrangements and the greater its per capita travel cost differences within the corporation. With airline rate deregulation and increased hotel price dealing, the less knowledgeable about prices the traveling executives, their secretaries, and in-house travel officers became. Financial officers of the corporations had little or no knowledge of the size of their annual travel costs corporatewide. The numbers were buried under other line items in the various budgets. By helping the corporation establish travel expense rules for each class of its travelers and then offering to handle all of a corporation's travel arrangements through a single dedicated American Express "travel desk" with a separate 800 telephone number dedicated to each corporation, American Express was able to help "control" travel costs corporatewide. It was able to search and bargain for the lowest possible rates, the lowest-cost routes, and the lowest-cost hotel accommodations within each class of lodging. It sent monthly systemwide travel cost analyses to the central financial officers, with flagged indicators of deviations from the travel expense rules. American Express was able to demonstrate that, even after charging its regular fees for Corporate Cards, it could save companies with normal annual travel budgets over $30 million at least 10 percent.

American Express looked at the world "out there" through the eyes of people whose needs it understood totally—the eyes of the corporate controllers of the purse strings. Controllers knew that costs of all kinds have a general tendency to creep up. They were increasingly concerned about the price of money. Knowing a lot about travel and travel-related costs, American Express asked itself simply: "How can we help the keepers of the corporate purse strings to manage costs that we know a lot about?" The rest wasn't easy but would never have been done had American Express not first done what was uniquely imaginative: combining disparate facts about its corporate customers and itself in ways that yielded new questions and previously unexperienced insights.

The essence of competition, as we have seen, is differentiation: providing something different and providing it better than your competitor. Sometimes even an obvious functional difference doesn't sell unless it is also presented or positioned differently. We know this from cosmetics and many other consumer goods. We saw it in the DuPont example. But consider computers. The explanation of Apple Computer's roaring success is not simply the enormous power it packed into minuscule size at a remarkably low price. Why would anybody, even at the price, and knowing all the horror stories of troubles with computers, buy this diminutive looking toy from this obscure company? The software available for Apple users was also usable on the minicomputers of Digital Equipment, Data General, Prime, and IBM. The genius of Apple was to avoid positioning itself as a new minicomputer, or even a microminicomputer. It did something entirely different. It called itself a "personal computer." It thus avoided having to assert itself as being yet another microminicomputer, only better, which would have required a claim of being merely superior to or cheaper than DEC, DG, or IBM. That, coming from obscurity, would have been hard to believe. Instead, Apple said, in effect, "We are an entirely new and different kind of computer—the newest new generation that the others don't have. We're different. It's a personal computer, intended for you as a normal person, not for the computer experts in your company."

Nowhere in recent years has the marketing imagination operated more powerfully to generate new customer-getting products than in financial services. Money-market mutual funds are the most spectacular example, providing access for people of modest means to balanced portfolios of high-interest-bearing and relatively secure commercial paper and making them available with enormous ease of purchase and redemption.

Another imaginative example are zero-interest, or money-multiplier, corporate bonds, issued at deep discounts from their redemption prices, requiring no periodic interest payments or related accounting costs for their issuers and incurring no tax liabilities for their owners until maturity. The remarkable ingenuity of the financial community became even more apparent when the invention of this security was almost instantly fol-

133

lowed by the emergence of a new category of zero-interest instruments in the form of regular bonds stripped of their coupons.

The passage of President Reagan's Economic Recovery Act of 1981 greatly raised the investment tax credits available to corporations. The financial community's quick ingenuity surfaced again. Within weeks corporations were selling their unused credits to others who could benefit from them.

While it may be said that designing and "manufacturing" a new financial instrument is much easier and cheaper than designing and manufacturing a new tangible product, and even that marketing it is relatively easier given the existence of highly flexible and well established electronic and direct-mail channels of distribution, two things help suggest that the American financial community is remarkably innovative nonetheless. First, these are uniquely American innovations. The developed financial communities of Western Europe and South America, facing high inflation for many years, did not invent any of these products. Second, neither did they invent or install the extensive electronic and direct-mail facilities that facilitated the management and distribution of these products. Though the American financial community does almost no market or consumer research, clearly some of its members have their own remarkably effective way of knowing what people out there want and value. Their way is the best way. It consists simply of letting themselves live, as it were, in their customers' shoes, talking their language, thinking their thoughts, feeling their emotions, responding to their cues. Most members of the financial community aren't like that, obviously. But it takes only a few who think this way to affect the entire industry. Once a new product was successfully introduced or a new channel of distribution successfully installed, swarms of imitators rushed in to transform everything that was done. It happened in insurance, commercial banking, credit cards, securities brokerage, options trading, mortgage banking, savings banking, and others.

The entrepreneurial vigor and audacity that have characterized the financial services industry in the past decade represent a diametrical departure from its former somnambulance. Mostly it started with the advent of new players on the scene or a handful of old players with new ideas, most especially people like Walter Wriston of Citicorp, Donald Regan of Merrill Lynch, and Jack Stein of the Dreyfus Fund. And there can be no doubt that it is they, as individuals, rather than their staffs or line subordinates, who personally made the revolutions associated with their companies. They had the visions, promulgated the ideas, and inspired their organizations. Besides the necessary vision and the facilitating determination and persistence, they also had the required daring. Anciently obtuse laws and regulations that stood obdurately against competitiveness and progress in the industry represented for these men things that had merely to be circumvented or changed, not, as with so many others, to be passively respected or merely criticized. Citicorp's invention of certificates of deposit and Merrill Lynch's invention of cash management accounts were end runs against obsolete and unrealistic regulations. And for neither of these firms were these isolated, one-time inventions. They were part of a continuing series of similarly shrewd and imaginative innovations. In both cases they were pieces of a transforming mosaic for their respective companies. They typify the centrality of marketing in corporate affairs. Decisions far at the top were based on shrewd insights regarding customer-getting possibilities far out in the field.

Let us repeat: The purpose of a business is to get and keep a customer. Without customers, no amount of engineering wizardry, clever financing, or operations expertise can keep the company going. To be the low-cost producer of vacuum tubes, to have the best salesmen of what's not wanted or wanted only by the few whose ability to pay won't even pay for the overhead —these can't save you from extinction. To do well what should not be done is to do badly.

What should be done can be defined only by reference to what customers do, can do, or might do in the market place. No amount of imagination can bail out companies intent on inappropriate purposes. The history of all succeeding and successful companies is a history of right purposes at the right times, executed with means right for their situations. Nor is selecting growth sectors on which to concentrate company effort a solution to the problem of stagnation. A lot of other companies are likely to have hit on the same target opportunities. The trick is to know how to convert opportunity into disproportionately opportune results. This means getting an edge over the other competitors.

The low-cost producer who gets disproportionate market share by passing part of his advantage along in the form of customer-getting lower prices has a clear and powerful advantage. But it must also be linked to doing everything else that's needed to satisfy the insatiably expanding wishes and demands of the market. In time, lower prices get taken for granted. What's usually wanted next are increasingly expanding clusters of other benefits and also often increasingly varied lines of product and service options for the customer. The strategy of price competitiveness makes sense only in the context of the larger or different clusters of things customers want and value. The trick is to combine price competitiveness with competitiveness in all other respects. In short, the trick is to provide the most competitive value.

All this is affirmed by one of the most interesting pieces of business scholarship in the last decade, by Professor William K. Hall of the University of Michigan, who is now at Cummins Engine Company. He studied the financial performance of leading firms in eight established old industries. Four were in consumer goods: automotive, major home appliances, brewing, and cigarettes; and four in industrial goods: steel, tire and rubber, heavy-duty trucks, and construction equipment. He discovered that over a significant period of time the leading firms in these industries outperformed such known growth-industry leaders as Phillips Petroleum among the oils; Xerox, Eastman Kodak, Texas Instruments, and Digital Equipment among the technology leaders; and General Electric and United Technologies among the diversification leaders. They even did better than IBM and 3M. The performance measures used by Professor Hall were average return on equity, average return on capital, and average annual revenue growth rate.[1]

[1] William K. Hall, "Survival Strategies in a Hostile Environment," *Harvard Business Review*, September/October 1980.

The unglamorous old basic-industry companies that did so well were National Steel, Michelin tires, Paccar trucks, John Deere farm equipment, Daimler Benz automobiles, Maytag washing machines, Heileman Brewing, and Phillip Morris cigarettes. The explanation of their superior performance was that they systematically went for meaningful differentiation in their offerings. "Differentiation" was objective both with regard to their generic products (see Chapter 4) and with respect to the rest of their total product, such as the nature and extent of such nontangible offerings as postpurchase servicing, parts availability, advisory help, delivery conditions and reliability, and the like. They understood the concept of the augmented product.

Hall further discovered that when these differentiation-oriented basic-industry high-performance companies were compared with their direct low-cost producer competitors, the former outperformed the latter. In short, meaningful differentiation is competitively more effective and enduring than low-cost production alone. When the two strategies were combined in a single company, such as by Caterpillar Tractor, the results were spectacular.

All this tells a simple and compelling story: Business success is a matter of the disproportionate and enduring attraction of certain proportions of customers at certain enduring levels of relative price. Most significantly, it is a story that defines the purpose of business in terms of marketing—once again, getting and keeping customers. This therefore installs marketing at the center of what's done in corporate strategic planning.

Strategic planning involves defining what's to be done, the allocation of resources for their maximization. Maximization is, and must inevitably be, getting the desired results in the market place. As we saw, being the low-cost producer, though enormously important, is hardly sufficient when focused on the wrong products, wrong distribution channels, and without regard to the wider wants of those segments. To decide correctly what's to be done and how to do it requires having good data about customers, competitors, and markets. Even more, it requires the imaginative conversion of these data into meaningful and usable information. The best way is to know your prospects

137

in a way that is more fundamental and compelling than what's usually yielded by the purely metrical methods so common in market research today.

The difference between data and information is that while data are crudely aggregated collections of raw facts, information represents the selective organization and imaginative interpretation of those facts. This requires knowing, in some sort of direct and systemic way, the world with which one presumes to deal. It requires getting inside the lives and work of the people one is trying to understand. Crudely aggregated collections of data merely represent what's been serially recorded about discrete events or categories. Information represents the imposition of order, categories, and ideas on the collected data. To do this merely by means of increasingly elaborate methods of statistical and mathematical refinement and calculation, whatever their merits, loses the throbbing pulse of the reality the data sought to capture. It's like assuming you know all about sex when you've read Masters and Johnson or *The Hite Report*.

Good data about customers, converted meaningfully into good information, have the power to improve strategic decisions in the right directions. Strategic planning can be mechanistically, and therefore incorrectly, defined as deciding how to allocate resources among the possibilities of what's to be done. This definition is incorrect, because it presumes that these possibilities are self-evident. They are not. It is wrong to say that the most important and creatively challenging act of corporate decision-making is about choices regarding what's to be done. The most important and challenging work involves thinking up the possibilities from among which choices may have to be made. To select among stipulated possibilities is to make choices of preferences, not decisions about appropriateness. A possibility has to be created before it can be chosen. Therefore to think up the possibilities from among which choices might be made is to engage in acts of creative imagination.

When Milton Greenberg of GCA Corporation focused on the possibilities of making different rather than improved capital equipment, he shoved his organization in a direction profoundly different from what would have been followed without that pur-

138

poseful nudge. The simple clarity of this different conceptualization as to what might be done was rooted totally in a profoundly simple and clear notion of what a large segment of the market basically wanted—even if the market itself did not know in advance exactly what it wanted. It was a strategic decision whose power resided in the creation of insightfully customer-oriented possibilities regarding what the choices were.

Strategic planning involves defining what's to be done. It is inescapably rooted in marketing matters, in the need to respond to the realities, the actualities of the market's unyielding requisites. To get done what strategic planning has decided to do requires realistic plans for implementation at the center of the competitive vortex. If the plans are not realistic, and if those who must convert the plans into action are not persuaded regarding their feasibility, the results will be disastrous. Subordinates will, perhaps grudgingly, carry out plans and programs they think are silly or wrong. But they will not seriously attempt to implement plans and programs they think are not realistic, that is, not implementable.

The Light Brigade moved obediently into the valley of death. Its own opinions regarding duty, rightness, appropriateness, or probable effectiveness were beside the point. So much for the world of the military arts. In the world of commercial affairs, duty is a lesser and less compelling calling. The plans and programs had better be reasonably right, appropriate, and compelling. They must be reasonably congruent with everyday common sense and, especially, easily understandable. In the absence of these, there is misunderstanding, resistance, and sometimes outright sabotage. People will not willingly or enthusiastically do what seems neither sensible nor suitable, and certainly not what's not understandable. They may not engage in outright opposition or sabotage, but they will drag their feet, communicate in various subtle ways to their peers and subordinates the absence of conviction or urgency, and tolerate sloppiness and slowness.

To be successful a strategy must also be simple, clear, and expressible in only a few written lines. If it is elaborate and complex, and takes a lot of space or time to communicate, few people will understand it or march to its tune. Complexity tends usually to mask a vague or unsubstantial sense of the realities that face the enterprise. The most dramatic and visible realities that so obviously destroy companies are usually fiscal: insufficient cash flow to finance debt and interest payments, to pay vendors, and the like. These usually make the headlines, because they lead so often and so obviously to bankruptcy. Often they are due to wrong decisions about purely financial affairs. Most commonly such wrong decisions are based on miscalculations or plain dumb assumptions about the market place—that sales would be sufficiently good, prices sufficiently high, accounts receivable sufficiently low and short-term. Hence, fiscal failure originates in the market place.

Marketing is inescapable in the determination of corporate results. The reason is that marketing deals with the sources and levels of the revenues that help determine the corporate fate. Since marketing means getting and keeping customers in some acceptable proportion relative to competitors, it is to the marketing imagination one must look to gain differential advantage over competitors. Assuming that the costs of what it sells are reasonably competitive, it remains the burden of the marketing imagination to find ways to attract and hold customers. It usually takes a lot of long and sweaty effort to get things done, and that itself may take a lot of imagination. But unless the decision as to what to do is appropriate, which is to say, unless it is imaginatively right, nothing can save the enterprise from disaster. Good work in pursuit of wrong purposes is more damaging than bad work in pursuit of right purposes. In business, the marketing imagination is the central tool for deciding on what the purposes are to be.

8

Marketing and Its Discontents

It seems impossible these days for people in marketing to gather anywhere in the world without the subject's finally turning to their troubles with the public. Everywhere marketing is maligned for its pushy, noisy, manipulative intrusions into our lives; its corruptive teachings of greed and hedonism; its relentless pursuit of the consumer's cash, regardless of consequence, save the profit of the seller.

Paradoxically, these complaints seem to rise in direct proportion to the rising practice of the marketing concept, that is, to the business implementation of the idea that success is most assured by responding in every fiscally prudent way to what people actually want and value. That is why market research is such a thriving industry.

Nothing characterizes the successful conversion in the past two decades of so many companies to the practice of the marketing concept than the rising criticism that they practice a baleful opposite. Thus, the more carefully companies try to "give the people what they want," the more surely they are attacked for trying to get people to buy what they don't want, what they don't need, and what they can't afford—and doing it with wanton waste, noise, abrasiveness, and vulgarity.

One might have assumed way back in those doleful days when Henry Ford made the famous remark, "They can have any color car they want, so long as it's black," that once business learned how to be more customer-oriented and less product-oriented, thus giving people any color they wanted, that today's greater responsiveness would create greater consumer satisfaction and certainly less criticism of business.

It hasn't worked out that way, in part for the same reason that the discovery of a new source of unlimited energy (atomic fission) has not made physics more popular. The marketing concept has spurred the professionalized study of people through market research. The psychologists, learning more about what motivates and actuates people in commercial matters than the people themselves know, have thus enabled business strategists to become what critics have called "hidden persuaders" and "captains of consciousness," turning with subterfuge and cunning to their advantage knowledge that in more innocent days we assumed would naturally produce a better world. This, too, has been the pattern in physics. Discovery becomes diabolized in use: The physicist in social action becomes seen as a sinister Dr. Strangelove, in possession of power to control the world, just as the psychologist in business becomes a devious "hidden persuader" with power to control the consumer.

About those who know a lot more than ourselves about things that can ruin our lives and ravage our pocketbooks, our defense is to attribute to them evil, or at least questionable, intent. In the case of business and marketing, the consumer's unease is understandable and perhaps even justified.

Consider again the basic premise of the marketing concept: that a company should determine what consumers need and want, and try to satisfy those wants and needs, provided that:

1. doing so is consistent with the company's strategy
2. the expected rate of return meets company objectives

Implicit in this are two further considerations:

1. A consumer need can generally be defined best in terms of a total marketing program (product, information, reassurance, distribution, attendant services, price, promotion), rather than simply the product itself.
2. Different consumers will want or need different things.

This latter idea we clarify into the concept of "market segments": that there are groups of potential customers sharing particular wants or needs (rather than that there is simply one large, gelatinous market), and that these groups are objectively identifiable.

The discovery of the idea of segments has become a powerful organizing principle in the affairs of modern business. Not that ancient business practitioners in Babylon did not know about segments—they did, selling different wares at different prices to princes than to paupers—but it never became an organizing principle that so consciously or fully dominated commercial life as it does now.

The objective difference between a prince and a pauper is in how much money each has. That is one of several demographic ways to distinguish between segments, rich and poor. It may also be the basis for social class and psychographic distinctions: elite versus mass, powerful versus powerless, self-assured versus self-doubting, psychologically independent versus dependent.

Translated into observable purchasing behavior, people may be segmented into their preferences for various product attributes. In automobiles, for example, some want a big car for the big family and some a smaller one for a small family with a limited budget; some prefer sporty speed to smooth-riding comfort; some will sacrifice certain comforts for lower operating costs; some want dual-purpose vehicles like station wagons to haul groceries and the little kids; while the teenage kids have dual purposes that are as quixotic as they are erotic.

The second category of segments deals with people's psychosocial wants and expressions—a car that reflects or affirms one's rank, position, achievement, or even aspiration, rather than his practical need (Rolls Royce, Cadillac); one that confirms a sense of power or command, one that suggests superior taste, or one that suggests freedom from susceptibility to commercial hucksterism.

These product and psychosocial segments can each be subdivided in an elaborate matrix of possibilities.

Since the marketing concept says that a company is likely to be more successful when it carefully determines and caters to the different wants and needs of different people, the practice of that concept explains a great deal that otherwise looks wasteful and baleful. If nothing else, it explains, for example, why we have so many different kinds of cars, and so many different kinds of laundry detergent with different chemical formulas, different brand names, and different advertising themes. Each targets a different little customer segment, even those detergents that are "all-purpose" and seek to appeal to the "I-don't-care, it-makes-no-difference-to-me" segment.

But for a lot of people it *does* make a difference. Some women want heavy-duty detergents that cut grease. Their husbands are automotive mechanics. Some, whose husbands are mechanics, may not want heavy-duty detergents because they degrade the fabric. Others want something that's safe for delicate underclothes, and others something that preserves or restores the original color. And, like cars, laundry detergents are also bought for psychosocial reasons. The appeal of a mild detergent may be that it affirms the buyer's self-perception of being of a superior species that has only beautifully delicate clothes, not all those tacky, tasteless rags of the lower classes. The appeal of a workhorse detergent that gets things "cleaner than clean" may affirm its user's undeviating dedication to the health and welfare of her family rather than seeming to be one of those fragile and frivolous jet-setters or one of those obsessed women's liberationists. Even the "all-purpose" buyer may in some

144

respects simply be saying "I'm above all that advertising idiocy. They can't fool me. Soap is soap."

When five major manufacturers of laundry detergents discover the existence of the same seven consumer segments, each having three groups of people who prefer their packages in a different size, we can quickly see why the supermarket has such a prodigality of brands and packages—in the United States, about 105 (5 producers × 7 segments × 3 packages = 105). And since the store doesn't want to go to the expense of refilling the shelves every few hours (which would, besides, inconvenience the shoppers), we not only get a lot of packages but a lot of shelf space devoted to them. All this, combined with all those ads, makes things look horribly wasteful.

But looked at another way, all this is merely the understandable consequence of competing producers and sellers responding to the wants, wishes, and behavior of various market segments. Whether this great proliferation of brands, packages, and advertising themes of products that are often only marginally different from one another (if not actually functionally identical), whether these "truly" satisfy consumer needs, or whether wants are being created where no needs "really" exist, or whether it is socially or economically desirable to "create" wants where consumers perceive no need until research discovers and capitalizes on them—these are the normative questions that underlie the issues.

The answers may be easy for some to give and agonizing for others. For both, they require one to act more or less as God's ventriloquist, declaiming on these rather trivial matters what's right or wrong, enough or too much.

The fact is, few of us actually need all of what we have or want. But once we've had our fill of simple food and shelter, can it honestly be said that everything else, including especially music, art, poetry, breathtaking cathedrals built at great expense to glorify God and humble man before Him, is unnecessary and perhaps even self-indulgent? Few of us in the more "advanced" nations will be satisfied to live, as Jesus Christus, in sackcloth and sandals. Nor, it seems, is anybody else who has a better choice. When T. S. Eliot said "Humankind cannot stand too

145

much reality,'' he meant to explain why in so many ways we try to escape nature's rude animality with manufactured shelter, man-made possessions, entertainments, arts, and fantasies. It's what we call ''civilization.''

We return to the paradox that puzzles and perplexes: Precisely as the marketing concept has advanced over the years, so, perversely, has the irritation it's produced, even among its practitioners. The millions of dollars annually spent on consumer research and product development, all designed to respond so carefully to what the consumer wants, do not stem the continuing assault on precisely the companies that seem most energetically, conscientiously, and effectively to spend that money.

It should come as no surprise that in recent years a lot of money has also gone into researching the reasons for the assault. Interestingly, there is surprisingly little complaining about product failures or deliberate excesses, like shoddy products, tricky warranties, deceptive advertising, misleading packaging, or questionable selling practices. While these surely exist, they are rare among the big visible companies, precisely those which sell their products the hardest and research their consumers the most. What seems to bug people most, even though they don't usually say it outright quite this way, is encompassed by the far less tractable and more serious charge of generalized wastefulness, offensiveness, and annoyance incident to so much marketing activity—the way it pollutes our lives.

A study by Professor Stephen Greyser of Harvard (reported in the *Journal of Advertising Research*) showed that 72 percent of the 2,500 American adults he surveyed felt advertising was more irritating than ten years before. Laundry soap and detergent ads were felt to be the most irritating. The big surprise is that the survey respondents consisted entirely of business executives. Imagine the results on the campus, at the League of Women Voters, or in the literary salons of the Western world.

But the study revealed something else that explains a lot: respondents were annoyed or offended by 37 percent of the ads for products they *did not* use but only 21 percent of those for products they *did* use. In other words, irritation and annoyance is produced not by the ads themselves but by their consumers as well. And that, really, is not such surprising news. Nobody is ever irritated by anything without his own consent. Indeed, the point is driven home hard in the study's disclosures about brands. Only 7 percent of the ads for one's favorite brand were disliked, as compared with 76 percent of the ads for competing brands. Whether these dramatically contrasting numbers are cause or effect is perhaps arguable. But other evidence and logic suggest a fairly clear answer. People like what they like and don't what they don't. They are most interested in what they think is more relevant to them than in what is not. They find comfort and reassurance and even flattery in ads for brands they've selected. If your family's soiled clothing is produced entirely by a husband and wife employed at sedentary jobs in air-conditioned offices, whose manual labor consists mostly of writing checks for theater tickets and country club dues, ads for heavy-duty detergents that remove grease from mechanics' overalls and grime from children's play clothes are likely to leave you irritated—maybe even highly distracted. If you are poor, ads for Adriatic cruises and Mercedes Benz automobiles will probably leave you frustrated. If you're healthy and athletic in all respects, ads for hemorrhoid relief will be distracting and probably offensive. But if your dentures slide, ads for new adhesives may be rather informatively welcome and helpful, though irritating and offensive to others. And if you've just bought a Winnebago motor home, its ads may be strongly reassuring that you've done the right thing, dispelling the usual post-purchase dissonance that research shows follows big expenditures. (The most avid and attentive consumers of auto ads are people who've just bought the brand being advertised. To keep your customers happy and coming back the next time around, it pays to advertise to those who have just bought, not just to those who might buy.) If you're looking for Granola or Special K ready-to-eat cereal, to have to search for it on a 60-foot triple-decker gondola loaded with children's brands like Cap'n Crunch and Froot Loops may leave you not only irritated but also exhausted.

Thus, in the case of consumer goods, which are the source of most of the irritations, complaints, and accusations, Steven Star points out that a lot of the trouble comes from the incongruence between the people for whom specific products, brands, and messages are specifically intended and the people who are exposed to them. The hemorrhoid ad is not particularly offensive to the afflicted viewer, reader, or listener. But most people exposed to the message aren't afflicted. Most likely they're either indifferent or offended. No matter how good Special K may be, toddlers will find the ads intrusive on their television watching, though ads for Cap'n Crunch may be received as informative, exciting, or titillating. Antismoking ads will probably irritate a lot of teenagers—another case of adults bugging them. And there are always too many gasoline stations, except for the person who is running low or has actually run out. Nor should we be surprised that laundry soap and detergent ads irritated the 2,500 executives most. How many of them do that household chore?

The incongruence between the intended and the actual audience for marketing programs represents an imperfection in the connection between the sophisticated practice of the marketing concept and the communications and institutions that facilitate marketing. To appreciate fully the resulting dilemmas and frustrations, it is useful to examine the ideas of marketing programs and segments a bit more fully.

A marketing program comprises the product; how it is packaged, priced, promoted, delivered; where it is sold; and so forth. Marketing programs are directed toward market segments. Indeed, the marketing concept almost by definition divides customers into many specific segments, regardless of product class, whether consumer goods, industrial goods, durable goods, capital goods, or consumables. A segment is that part of the population that has the need in question that might be satisfied with a particular product and marketing program. But some parts of that segment are not particularly good "fits" for every part of the marketing program. For example, some members of the segment may have the need for the indicated product but not the money to buy it. Some may have both but live too far from any place where the product can be economically delivered or serviced. Some may have the need, the money, and the proximity but not the interest. But all may be exposed to the marketing program—the ads for the product, its visible presence where they shop, or its appearance in use where they visit, work, or play. Those in need who are exposed but can't afford to pay will be frustrated. Those in need who are exposed and who *can* afford to pay but have no interest may be distracted. Both may be irritated, as, indeed, will those who found the communication or program highly interesting yesterday and bought, but having bought are now exposed to redundant messages. Having made their choice, they now feel badgered.

It is thus no surprise that irritation, frustration, and distraction arise most commonly in connection with consumer goods marketing. Here is the widest and most frequent incongruity between the total audience exposed to a marketing program and the specific "best fit" proportion of the market segment being targeted. A million people may be exposed to the marketing program (the ads, the displays in the shops), though it is designed for the segment needs of only 400,000, and the "best fit" of only 100,000 of that segment. This 100,000 "best fit" becomes the actual "Program Target"—the only one that can conceivably become satisfied by the marketing program. The other 90 percent who get the message are bored, irritated, distracted, frustrated, or some combination of these. And if some proportion of the best fit 10 percent has already bought the offered product, they too will be bored or irritated.

Such incongruence and abrasion is much less likely in industrial goods. Potential customers are often relatively few, with each representing potentially large sales volume. Customers who share a particular need (a market segment) are likely to group themselves into clearly identifiable targets (say, all companies that anodize metal). Finally, there are highly specialized trade media through which to reach them: magazines, industry conventions, distribution channels. The congruence of market segment, marketing program, and program target with the audience exposed to the marketing program is likely to be considerable. Things get organized to make them that way. Thus IBM

149

effectively divided its data processing business into sixteen major market segments (banking, distribution, aerospace, education, medical, government, and so on). A separate program was developed for each segment, and individual salesmen and sales offices were specialized by individual segments. The customer got the communications and programs suited to his special needs. Overlap and incongruence were minimal.

Not so, however, in consumer goods. All business is aware of the problem, though not often sufficiently conscious of its awareness. The big advertisers who use the mass media, and especially television, consider them the cheapest effective ways of reaching mass markets. Yet they tend generally to go to a lot of effort to mitigate the incongruities they're aware of. No children's programs are put on television at 10:00 P.M. Radio news reports, sponsored by ads for men, get heavily aired during commuting hours. Most general interest magazines in the larger countries carry regional editions whose advertising is tailored to those regions. Some general interest magazines do the same for such subscriber groups as medical doctors and teachers. Similarly, specialty stores carry only certain specialty products, like pharmaceuticals, sporting goods, and the like. All this mitigates incongruence and abrasion. But not a whole lot.

Though marketing tries increasingly to fashion products, communications, distribution channels, prices, and other components of the marketing mix to suit the special needs and capabilities of carefully defined market segments, thus giving the customer more nearly what he wants, this fashioning, notwithstanding increasingly specialized targeting activities, inescapably creates more irritated, frustrated, and distracted consumers. The best intentions, supported by the best efforts, return abrasion and hostility.

Direct marketing via mail, telephone, and cable can help mitigate this unhappy condition. In direct marketing, products, messages, and even media can be specifically tailored and even limited to their intended audiences. Best-fit program targets can be more closely matched to precise program audiences. The better this can be done, the more effective it will be as a marketing device, and the more attractive its relative costs to its user. It may cost more but still be cheaper.

Much depends on getting the fit right, of course, but the fit will almost always be better than with most mass media. Hence it has the potential of reducing social dissonance while also improving marketing effectiveness. But, as with most things, a good thing is not necessarily improved by its multiplication. An abundant daily harvest of unsolicited direct mail, no matter how interested I am in collecting stamps or improving my sexual performance, can get to be too much. The phone can ring too often and too inconveniently with invitations to ski where the skiing is best, buy where the price is lowest, and get what's not easily available elsewhere. This is not to mention the irritations of these calls when in incompetent hands, or the trickiness, pushiness, and effrontery of some of the mail.

When the marketing concept operates at full throttle, it generates products, services, and communications that target the specifically discovered needs and wants of specific narrow best-fit consumer segments. Each segment therefore has a better chance of getting what it really wants or needs than in the bad old days when Henry Ford told people they could have any color Model T they wanted so long as it was black.

But there are costs. One, production runs are shorter, distribution channels more varied and more crowded, and prices probably higher. Two, while more people are better satisfied by getting a chance to buy what's better tailored to their specific functional or psychosocial wants, an almost exactly equal number of people get frustrated, annoyed or distracted by the marketing programs of what they don't want, or can't afford but would like to have. Add to this the fact that the sheer magnitude of commercial communications is expanded as product numbers increase and that it is intensified through emulation and competitive drive. Put them all together, and one begins to see the reason for the perverse simultaneity of a triumphant marketing concept that seeks better to satisfy the public and a less satisfied public.

Or so it seems. The disjunctions, abrasions, and irritations

I've referred to certainly exist. But something else also exists: the apparent insatiability of human appetites, regardless of how much better off they keep getting. Each generation everywhere seems to ask for what its predecessors asked only of God. The special condition of present times is that we have all so suddenly been immersed in such an intensively communicative world that we have become intensely conscious of all the squalor, greed, competitiveness, dishonesty, negation, and covetousness that have, in fact, characterized humankind from the beginning. A rereading of the Old Testament or the Iliad quickly reminds us of how much each told us about the awful presence in their times of these rather ignoble human traits. It takes a Geiger counter to find any alleviating traces in either book of any continuing evidence of civic virtue, honor, civility, humanity, self-denial, and decency. They surface mostly as contrasting examples of how things might or ought to be rather than how they were.

In past times we excelled not in civic virtue or nobility of character but in ignoring, hiding, disguising, and denying the prodigal existence of their infamous opposites.

Today these are harder to bury or ignore, in part because, for the moment at least, we seem to take a special masochistic pleasure in parading our imperfections in public view every hour of the day. Also, because we're doing so well, exceptions to our good fortunes become by contrast more visible as well as more irritating. In the dark and desperate 1930s, with 25 percent unemployment that lasted for ten years, and before unemployment compensation, Social Security, Medicare, HUD, and pot, good fortune was to be able to hold one's job, any job, or failing that, to get on the WPA. In the affluent 1980s, when unemployment is way less, with home ownership, auto ownership, education, medical services, and symphony attendance way up, one still hears the self-abusing insistence that "we can do better."

In those despairing 1930s the nation enjoyed the greatest effulgence of wit and humor it had ever seen—Benchley, Thurber, George Kaufman, Dorothy Parker, E. B. White, and popular funnymen like Jack Benny, Fred Allen, Eddie Cantor, Burns and Allen, Fibber McGee and Molly, Amos and Andy, Charlie McCarthy. In the affluent 1980s we are treated in contrast to a grating specter of gloom and glumness, with half the public pundits saying that decay and decadence have destroyed our spirit and our capabilities, and the other half, as I said, that "we can do better."

We have noted that nothing characterizes success so much as its attendant miseries. We now see that marketing, one of mankind's less cosmic concerns for urgent attention, may be no exception to that apparent rule. We focus in our lives and in public affairs more on what's wrong, bad, corrupt, and unfinished than on what's accomplished, good, noble, alleviating, and progressing. More than two hundred years ago Edward Gibbon wrote, "There exists in human nature a strong propensity to depreciate the advantages, and to magnify the evils of present times." It is still so. The end of the world is not at hand.

Nor is there any presumption that if we solve all our known problems and remove all basis for discontent, then we shall at last be happy. The problem is that every solution creates new problems.

9

Addendum on Management and the Postindustrial Society

As if the world's industrial nations didn't already have enough troubles, for some years now we have been offered a new malady that shatters whatever slight faith remains in the meliorating possibilities of abundance. This is to the effect that we are entering a world of economic entropy: The more economically advanced that nations become, the less their living standards will rise until, finally, those standards begin to fall.

Advanced goods-producing nations, it is said, become goods-satiated and service-hungry. As affluence waxes, the demand for goods wanes. A third family car seems less urgently needed than the second; after one refrigerator, another is a marginal convenience. On the other hand, the demand for travel, education, entertainment, eating out, health care, and other services accelerates both absolutely and relatively. More of the nation's work shifts from the production worker to the lower-level service worker and the upper-level "knowledge worker," whose activities have only limited access to the kinds of industrial and science-based technologies that so profoundly increased productivity in manufacturing and farming in the last hundred years. Hence costs and prices rise more rapidly, and a structural malignancy increasingly creeps into the economy. As we want relatively more of the things that cost relatively more to produce, the less well-off we shall become. Thus the anomaly of our age: Economic progress "immiserizes" itself.

The most sophisticated version of this gloomy prognosis is contained in the account of the coming "postindustrial" society, which elaborately describes the nature and consequences of this structural shift from a production to a service economy.[1] This account is indeed based on some facts and is, on its face, plausible enough.

In the past twenty years, the non-goods-producing sector of the United States nonagricultural labor force expanded much faster than the goods-producing sector. Civilian government employment alone rose four times the rate of goods-producing equipment. While the growing numbers of service and knowledge workers (retail and office clerks, janitors, repairmen, waiters, scientists, teachers, government employees, and professional and technical workers in medicine, health care, law, and the like) are said to plod ingloriously to produce about as much today as they did twenty years ago, the output of industrial workers expands with the help of CAD/CAM equipment, robots and factory systems, cybernetic controls, and fluid processors. As industrial productivity rises, so do industrial wages. Unless the incomes of service workers also rise, they will suffer from the unequal distribution of productivity gains. But their incomes *do* rise. In the past twenty years their real incomes have risen nearly as fast as those of industrial workers. Salaries of federal government employees rose an average of nearly 9 per-

[1] Daniel Bell, *The Coming of Post-Industrial Society: A Venture in Social Forecasting* (New York: Basic Books, 1973), especially Chaps. 2 and 3. A more succinct and also unqualified statement of the economic consequences of this structural shift is in Bell's essay, "Changing Influences in American Life," *Business and Society in Change* (New York: American Telephone and Telegraph Co., 1974), pp. 65–82. Most of the references in this chapter are to the 1973 book.

cent a year, salaries of local police and firemen about 7 percent a year, and salaries of industrial production workers only 6 percent a year. But since service *productivity* presumably lags substantially, rising service wages force everybody to share the consequent inflation and lowered standards of living.

The "postindustrial" society thus seems to be in the malignant grip of its own differential achievements and conflicting desires. Uneven productivity rates and the rapid expansion of the less productive sector create a structural "cost-push" inflation. This in turn is inflamed by what Daniel Bell calls a "revolution of entitlements," the crescive insistence that government should assure everybody a wide range of minimum rights and benefits.

Bell concludes that this "structural . . . problem . . . can be overcome only by somehow finding methods to increase productivity in the service sector." In this conclusion he is joined by many others. Peter Drucker writes flatly, "The only feasible solution to our economic problem is to raise productivity, and the only way to accomplish this is by raising the productivity of knowledge work," that is, the work of the upper service ranks, the "managers, engineers, computer programmers, or medical technologists . . . the skilled and semiskilled knowledge workers who are where the growth is and is going to be." Similarly, the President's National Commission on Productivity, made up of practical men of affairs from the upper echelons of business, agriculture, and labor, declared in its 1971 policy statement that "there has been lagging productivity growth within . . . government, the various services, construction, trade, finance, insurance, and real estate" and that their underperformance threatens "a higher standard of living and a better quality of life."

SERVICE PRODUCTIVITY

The problem, then, is whether it is possible to make the service economy in the twentieth century as productive as manufacturing became in the nineteenth century. "How can we do it?'' Drucker asks, and responds: ''No one has any answers . . . .'' Most people seem to believe there is no answer. Fortunately there is.

First, however, some moderating propositions: (1) The goods-producing fecundity of industrial society has not been homogeneous—its productive prowess has been exaggerated; (2) the productive advances of the service sector have been widely understated and its potentials badly underestimated; and (3) government employment, the most heavily labor-intensive portion of the service sector, though in explosive growth since 1960, is now visibly headed for both a proportional and an absolute decline. Finally, and this is the heart of the matter, the gloomy account of a low-productivity service economy is rooted in an almost wanton disregard of the historical role and future possibilities of the managerial arts for improving labor productivity.

If these propositions are right, the supposed consequences of the supposedly unique structure of the ''postindustrial'' society are far less real or worrisome than advertised. Nobody really disagrees about the need for more productivity in the service sector. *Fortunately we are getting it, we know why, and we know how to get more.*

What is crucially missing in most assessments concerning the possibility of increasing service-sector productivity is any serious consideration of exactly what accounts for the great productivity of the goods-producing industries. We are offered only confident and conventional assertions, based largely on orthodox but unexamined dogma and very little on any analysis of actual historical situations. Indeed, the conventional ''facts'' about what produced the magnificent thrusts of productivity in the goods-producing sectors are largely ''factoids,'' merely imaginary as regards historical facts and their relative importance. Overlooked is what I shall argue was specifically the most important element in the success of the industrial age: the element of ''management.''

Ignoring the role of management in the growth of industrial systems *ipso facto* exaggerates the importance of machines and the artifacts of production. Since those machines and artifacts are not presumed to be present or easily usable in service industries today, gloomy conclusions are understandably reached about the future productivity of the expanding service sector, and therefore about the future living standards of the "post-industrial" society.

On the other hand, if the enormous abundance of the industrial age was the product not of new technology but rather of the art of management—that strangely neglected and often rudely dismissed field of activity—then one must consider whether management could also play such a fructifying role in the service economy. I believe that it can and that evidence in favor of this thesis is already plentiful.

THE ROLE OF MANAGEMENT

Management as a practical art originally developed in the conduct of war. Even today tables of organization and the language of industrial management derive from the military concepts of "line" and "staff." The Industrial Revolution gradually adopted and expanded these concepts and procedures. Today management is understood and acknowledged as the unique and central characteristic of that revolution by those who really know the inner workings of modern industry. Management is *the* primary engine of progress, as progress is generally defined. The crucial importance of management has been eclipsed by the historians' almost obsessively childlike fascination with the technological artifacts of nineteenth-century industry and the flamboyant entrepreneurs of that era. But the precise story of how those entrepreneurs rendered those artifacts—the machines, engines, tools, and crude instruments—productive has not been properly told to this day. Neither Lewis Mumford nor Max Weber—and certainly not Karl Marx—ever bothered to explore the specific details of the functional roles played by industrial organizers and managers.

The significance of management in the creation and development of the industrial age can perhaps best be understood by noting how long it took for the available technology actually to create that age. Technologically speaking, the industrial age began in Milan around 1335, with the gear-driven time clock. It contained all the mechanical hardware and engineering know-how we associate with the machinery of the Industrial Revolution in the nineteenth century. But it took Eli Whitney, in New Haven in 1798, to wrest the available technology from the dead hands of isolated medieval craftsmen and put it into the more productive hands of organized unskilled labor. Whitney's contribution was less technological than managerial. To assemble interchangeable musket parts, he created large-scale factories where there had been one-man shops; he organized, directed, and controlled groups of workers to do with existing technologies what had previously been done singly and alone.

It took more than four hundred years to go from the clock to the musket factory, and Whitney's contribution was precisely the work of what we call today the "manager." He was also an entrepreneur, but that part of his activity has almost totally obscured a more arduous and encompassing aspect—his role as a serious organizer and manager.

Management consists of the rational assessment of a situation and the systematic selection of goals and purposes (what is to be done?); the systematic development of strategies to achieve those goals; the marshaling of the required resources; the rational design, organization, direction, and control of the activities required to attain the selected purposes; and, finally, the motivating and rewarding of people to do the work. Whitney's idea of interchangeable parts for manufacturing muskets might be said—in the profundity of hindsight—to have led "inescapably" to the creation of the mass production factory. But it was hardly obvious then—nor was it, in fact, a century later. Henry Ford's singular contribution was not that he invented, or even reinvented, the assembly line. He didn't. He merely rediscovered it while witnessing the operation of Julius Rosenwald's Sears, Roebuck mail-order warehouse in Chicago, where roving clerks assembled orders by picking items off the shelves. Ford's unique insight was that the potential buyer's real problem was getting enough money to buy a car, and he set out to solve that problem by finding a way to make cars more cheaply. (On the other hand, Ford might have invented install-ment credit to solve the problem—a "solution" that came later.) The solution derived largely from Ford's seminal reconceptual-ization of the engineering of the automobile, making it an assem-bled rather than a constructed machine. If he had not redesigned the automobile as an assembly of parts, it could not have been manufactured on an assembly line, where the shift from inde-pendent craftsmen working alone to unskilled multitudes work-ing together under highly ordered and closely supervised conditions helped control quality, productivity, and costs.

The functional rationality that characterizes the cognitive mode of management makes a difference. Technology is not enough. It is one of the great modern mysteries that, although so much is owed by our times to the organizing and productive genius of management, the world must constantly be reminded of this fact, which it seems so obstinately reluctant to learn and believe. And, curiously, it is precisely in the world's intellectual enclaves—in the universities and among writers and journalists —that this obstinacy reaches its apex. Somehow results are pre-sumed to happen as if by immaculate conception. It is well to appreciate what the absence of good management can mean in our daily lives. For example, it is a fact now unanimously ac-knowledged by those who understood that, after the Arab oil embargo in November 1973, it took only one week of intensive round-the-clock work by the managers of the oil industry to rearrange completely the entire sourcing, shipping, pipelining, and delivery of the world's oil and petroleum products to get things back on a new, functioning track. I have been told per-sonally by extremely high-placed government officials in Eu-rope, the United States, and Japan that they viewed this as an almost miraculous achievement that none of the governments themselves could conceivably have accomplished. Compare this with the pathetic logistical blunder in late 1975—by Nigerian government officials well trained in economics at the best British universities—that resulted in a massive glut of 120 cement-laden cargo ships in Lagos harbor with no place to dock and no space or little use for their loads.

Or consider the venerable business of manufacturing textiles and wearing apparel. In 1969 Czechoslovak labor productivity in these industries was 56 percent above that of Hungary. For every hundred workers needed to do the job in Hungary, only sixty-nine were needed in Czechoslovakia. Each Czech worker, aided by more machinery than the Hungarian worker, consumed 4,080 kilowatt hours of electricity a year, as against 3,108 for the Hungarian worker. But though the Czech worker consumed on the average 31 percent more electricity, he produced 56 percent more goods. It is not that the Czech electric machinery was more modern or that there was more of it; it was that the manufacturing process was better managed. Understandably, even though the state rules both economies, the Czech citizen pays less for his clothes than does the Hungarian. In the end, it is the nature and quality of management that makes the real difference.

VARIATIONS IN PRODUCTIVITY

In order to assess the possible effects of a shift to a service economy, it is necessary to have a clear picture of the realities of the goods-producing economy.

The amount of capital per employed worker in an industry is an accepted measure of the level of its industrialization. The difference between the value of the materials used and the value of what results from the manufacturing process measures the "productivity" (or "value added") of those employed in the effort. "Value added" per employed person is the accepted measure of labor productivity. The automobile assembly line is the prototypical example of the productive rewards of replacing human with machine effort. But compared with oil refining, auto manufacturing is a backward industry. Even a decade ago, in 1972, the United States oil industry used $173,000 in plant, equipment, and other assets for every single one of its workers; the motor vehicle industry used $22,600. The "value added" per oil refinery employee was $41,600. Per motor vehicle plant it was only $22,500 per employee, relatively greater but absolutely less than in refining. In the fabricated metals industries (which are heavy suppliers of parts and subassemblies to the auto, machine tool, trucking, railroad, and other important technology-based industries) the "value added" per employee was only $18,200. While the investment per fabricated metals employee was $146,930 lower than in the oil industry, it was also $6,000 less than in the food-manufacturing industry. Obviously, the goods-producing sector of the American economy is neither homogeneously capital-intensive nor uniformly productive.

The industrial society we knew prior to World War II, which remains in declining dominance today, was the creation of what Daniel Bell refers to as "inspired tinkerers": Whitney, McCormick, Ford, Kettering, and even Alexander Graham Bell. They symbolize the triumph of trial-and-error mechanics over raw nature. Now we have the ascendance of science-theoretical knowledge over practical knowledge. Or so it is claimed. Daniel Bell explains: "The science-based industries of the 1970s—electronics, optics, polymers—begin and end with theoretical knowledge. Consequently . . . knowledge becomes an extraordinary strategic resource." There the new productive leverage is supposed to lie, and it does—to a degree. Consider the computer: Starting with Univac in 1952, it is already in its fifth generation. Since 1952, every seven years there has been a tenfold increase in electronic computing speed and productivity. All this is presumed to be the work of "science."

But is it that simple? The production of integrated circuits and microprocessors (the heart of the new generation of computer electronics) starts with the design of a desired set of circuits. The design, it is true, ultimately derives from a body of theory, or "pure" knowledge. However, the designing itself is laboriously done by engineers on a CAD tube. These designs are photographically reduced and reproduced by means of a pattern generator that creates a master mask, which is then multiplied in vast numbers ("chips") onto single crystal wafers by means of a photorepeater. Yet both the pattern generator and the photorepeater are themselves manufactured singly by skilled craftsmen working in a manner not much different from that of the medieval clockmaker in effort, attention to metal-working precision, and solitary pride. The runners on which the photorepeater's filming equipment moves are constructed by crafts-men who laboriously grind, sand, and polish metal by hand for days, an effort much like the finishing of the world's most pow-erful telescope by technicians from Holland, who entered their apprenticeship at age fourteen. If you measure productivity by the metal shavings and dust the craftsman produces, he cannot compare even with the unskilled worker of 1856 who operated a pedal-driven mechanical grinding wheel in the McCormick reaper plant in Chicago. Yet such a craftsman, whose education was probably limited to a vocational high school in Muncie, Indiana, is a crucial member of that superlatively efficient, science-based knowledge industry, electronics.

The manufacturing of the microcircuit chips and micropro-cessors is by any modern measure the least efficient of indus-tries. A plant is regarded as highly efficient if it yields 5 percent usable output out of every batch "cooked" during the first year of a new circuit's production. In subsequent years, 20 percent is considered acceptable and 30 percent stupendous, almost mirac-ulous. The remainder are scrapped. What would we say of De-troit's technological might if seventy out of every hundred cars coming off the assembly line had to be scrapped at the factory?

Bell declares that science-based industries "begin and end with theoretical knowledge." Begin, yes, but not end. Who are considered among the most valued workers in the integrated circuit industry? The handful of people who run the "ovens" that "cook" the chips and microprocessors. They are almost regarded as alchemists, possessing arcane skills that cannot be transmitted by observation or learned by university study. "Learning" is by trial and error, and things often go inexplic-ably awry even for the possessors of the secret formulae, care-fully recorded in heavily guarded recipe books. No wonder that the most despicable crime in this most "scientific" of knowledge industries is the piracy of a "cooker," a person whose value derives not from theoretical knowledge or college education but from the same kind of artful (even "primitive") tinkering typical of Whitney, McCormick, and Kettering. True, without prior de-velopments in theoretical knowledge, the "cookers" would never have had a chance to learn their practical arts. True also that Dr. Charles H. Townes could not have invented the laser without the theoretical knowledge of optics, physics, and advanced electromechanics. The situation now is wholly different from what it was in the time of Thomas Edison, who achieved spectacular results although he was not familiar with the works of Michael Faraday and others. Conditions *have* changed. We *are* more dependent on knowledge than before. But we ought not to exaggerate that dependence.

Though the integrated circuit, the child of theoretical knowledge, is capable of enormous productivity and can be more efficiently produced relative to its performance capabilities than its predecessor, the transistor, its manufacturing process (as well as that of the microprocessor) contradicts the lyrical claims made for the productive advances of the more sophisticated goods-producing industries. Thinking things up is not the same as making things happen. It is not merely that there still are a lot of slips between the cup and the lip. It is simply that though science-based industries may begin with theoretical knowledge, they do not *end* with it. Translation of knowledge into results is almost purely a matter of "tinkering" and, more importantly, a matter of management.

The gap between the scientific origins and the technological practices of the electronics industry is a microcosm of all others. The goods-producing sector is not homogeneously productive on all fronts, not even within given "standard industrial classification" categories. It may seem permissible to generalize about the differences between goods-producing and service-producing sectors in the rates of productive advances, but such generalization is both unwarranted and misleading. Back in 1973, the year Bell published his "postindustrial society" book, John W. Kendrick, America's eminent "productivity" scholar, published studies showing the following annual rates of productivity increases in U.S. manufacturing industries between 1948 and 1966: foods, 3.0 percent; beverages, 2.2 percent; tobacco, 1.1 percent; paper, 2.5 percent; chemicals, 4.9 percent; stone, clay, and glass, 2.4 percent; primary metals, 1.6 percent; electric machinery, 3.7 percent. In a previous study for the period 1899–1953 his calculations showed the following average annual rates of increase: foods, 1.7 percent; beverages, 1.6 percent; tobacco,

3.5 percent; paper, 2.3 percent; chemicals, 2.9 percent; stone, clay, and glass, 2.6 percent; primary metals, 1.9 percent; electric machinery, 2.2 percent.

Obviously, the rates are not homogeneous within manufacturing or between time periods. And this is the case outside the United States as well. A 1972 United Nations study showed that the relative productivity per employed person in manufacturing industries exhibited wide variations. In 1969 France was 29.9 percent above Czechoslovakia, Czechoslovakia 17.8 percent above Austria, and Austria 57 percent above Hungary. What seems clear is that productivity varies not only among manufacturing industries and nations but by stages in industrial life cycles as well.

UTILIZING TECHNOLOGY

To speak of the goods-producing sector as more "productive" or more steadily expanding in productive efficiency than the service-producing sector is to enlist a few facts into an excessively encompassing generalization.

Between 1899 and 1953 the average annual productivity increase in the United States railroads was 2.6 percent; in local transit, 2.5 percent; in telephone service, 2.0 percent. Each of these *service* industries did better during that half-century than industries manufacturing foods, beverages, apparel, lumber products, leather products, primary metals, nonelectric machinery, and furniture.

Though service productivity has generally lagged behind goods productivity, what distinguishes the better-performing service industries is the enormous help they get from technology. The capital invested in America's railroads rose each year (save four) from 1869 to 1931. In 1931 the real (that is, adjusted for price changes) new investment in the railroad industry, in spite of proliferating bankruptcies, was still 5 percent above the 1889 figure. The capital invested in the telephone and telecommunications industries has risen dramatically each decade from 1879 until today.

Thus the great technological flowering of the industrial sector has also helped the service sector and in some cases has produced productivity expansion much more dramatic in the latter than in the former. There is no presumption that things will or must be different in the "postindustrial" society. Recent developments are, in fact, quite promising.

Victor R. Fuchs, the leading scholar on the productivity characteristics of service industries, has no trouble confirming that in the aggregate, the output per man-hour in the United States service sector is about half that of the manufacturing sector. But in recent decades service productivity has actually grown faster than manufacturing. Between 1929 and 1965, long before office and information automation made their big computerized leaps forward, the productivity growth of the industrial sector exceeded that of the service sector by an average of only 0.2 percentage points per year. The service industries had already begun to catch up. Indeed, in this same period the growth in two service industries actually exceeded the average of the whole manufacturing sector: Transportation was higher by 1.4 percentage points; communications and public utilities by 2.6 percentage points.

Those two were, of course, heavy beneficiaries of technology. But the technological achievements and possibilities in other service industries are widely unappreciated. Fuchs reports three case studies that help make the point. Consider beauty and barber shops. When the safety razor shifted shaving from the barber shop to the home, the demand for haircuts also declined, because men visited barber shops less frequently. This reduced the number of productive hours barbers spent during a given work day and the amount of the average transaction. Since these are indices of "productivity," the *measured* productivity of barbers declined, though not their efficiency or actual productivity. In beauty shops there was an opposite trend. With the development of better permanent-wave equipment and hair dyes, these services have increased both transaction size and traffic. The accelerated traffic stimulated the creation of even better and faster equipment and dyes, thus raising productivity and traffic even more. All this has been augmented by single transactions that increasingly combine women's haircuts and shampoos.

Now, with a sudden shift in men's hair fashions, the frequency of visits by men to barber shops has risen, as has the price of "hair styling" and, consequently, the productivity of barber shops.

ASSESSING MASS TRANSIT

These examples help explain the peculiar productivity figures in mass transportation. More people per capita now fly more planes more often than formerly took trains. Both the train and the plane created quantum increases in real efficiency over their respective predecessors. Yet railroad productivity suffers today, as did barber shops for a while, not because these industries work less well but because fewer people patronize them. Indeed, the measuring system systematically underreports the efficiency of railroads, as it does the efficiency of airlines, because it does not account for the value of time and money. Reuben Gronau's 1970 study for the National Bureau of Economic Research on the value of time in passenger transportation shows that for trips exceeding 176 miles, the time saved in flying relative to train or bus travel, though not measured as a benefit in conventional productivity calculation, adds an enormous increment to the results of that calculation. The plane today (like the train in the past) is thus even more productive in its new applications than is reported, if we include its positive externalities: the time freed for its users' other concerns and the value of money freed from financing the inventory of in-transit products.

The same is actually true of the relationship between public mass transportation and the private automobile. Productivity in mass transportation has declined because, for the most part, patronage has declined. But when the productivity of its alternative, the automobile, is measured in terms of the benefits perceived by its owners, the automobile clearly becomes more efficient even than a fully utilized subway. *Free Transit,* an exhaustive preference and attitude study of Boston area residents by Thomas A. Domencich and Gerald Kraft, shows the "almost complete insensitivity of (mass) transit's share of the market to such transit-system performance variables as its fare or times (i.e., speed)." The convenience, flexibility, and privacy of the automobile are what is valued, even given the substantially higher per-mile costs. No wonder San Francisco's elegant new BART transit system—quiet, comfortable, spacious, fast, running at frequent regular intervals, and now reasonably reliable, with big, free, well-lighted parking lots at suburban stations— operates far below its expected level, even with the higher operating costs of commuting by car.

And no wonder that the distinguished transit economist and historian George W. Hilton, in his 1974 study of the Urban Mass Transit Assistance program, said that almost all UMTA experimental programs were flops. No wonder that in a 1974 referendum Los Angeles area voters overwhelmingly rejected a proposed new 146-mile mass transit subway system. What they had—their cars—was better, even conceding the cost of the government support system (roads and police, for example) that "subsidize" the private automobile. (But the motorists are *not* subsidized. They pay taxes for what they get.) In the end, had the Los Angeles subway been built, its most notable contribution would have been a further reduction in the reported "productivity" rates of the nation's mass transit statistics. More technology would have produced less reported productivity because of underutilization. The problem with productivity statistics in the service sector is that they so often fail to measure the total benefits (the externalities, like time and convenience) and to account for shifts to new classifications (for example, from the live theater to the movies), or they are distorted by the underutilization that results from the choice of higher-valued, though not always more costly, alternatives.

When it is said that the "postindustrial" or knowledge-worker society can avoid inflation and the cannibalization of its own living standards only by making service somehow as productive as the technology-based and science-based industries, that is not wrong. But there is nothing inherently more productive about technology. If people don't want the output or resist machines *per se*, the yield of technology will be less, not more.

THE "PRODUCTIVITY PROBLEM"

Nor does it follow that service is inherently less capable of employing the technologies that, on the average, make manufacturing more productive than service. We have already noted some cases. On more familiar grounds, consider the movies: They vastly raised the productivity of actors who previously performed on stage, night after night, to a few hundred patrons. The same is true of television versus movies. If our productivity data were assembled in terms of the "entertainment sector" rather than its separate and descriptively arbitrary components, like "motion pictures" and "theater," the reported results would be vastly different. As things stand, the results look terrible, but the reality is pretty good: It is actually not the "theater" or the "movies" that people want, but "entertainment." The explosive advances that the movies and then television generated in units of entertainment productivity in their very infancy were geometrically greater than the increases made by such pioneers of industrial standardization and mass production as the manufacturers of muskets after the Revolutionary War or the manufacturers of army uniforms in the Civil War.

The "productivity problem" of the service industries is actually being "solved" more rapidly than it originally was in the goods-producing industries. As we have seen, it took more than four hundred years to go from the clock to Eli Whitney's musket factory. By that standard, the "productivity problem" in manufacturing took a very long time to be "solved." In contrast, the very first commercially produced computer instantly replaced the hand labor of thousands of inefficient and erratic office workers employed in the weekly preparation of corporate payrolls. But the resultant productivity improvements in this service activity did not appear in the statistics. They were buried (and still are) in the gross figures of the industries for which such payrolls are prepared.

The computer is an example of the substitution of productivity-enhancing technology for low-productivity service workers. Other examples are the substitution of coffee-vending machines for waitresses, automatic cash-vending machines for

169

bank tellers, and coin-operated travel insurance machines for clerks. In numerous other cases, technology enhances the productivity of people rather than totally substituting for them: typewriters to replace quills and ink; electroencephalograms (and now, electronic brain scanners) to increase the speed and accuracy of neurologists, neurosurgeons, and neuroradiologists; detergents and motorized equipment to increase the productivity, improve the quality of work, and alleviate the burden of scrubwomen; electric tools and electronic diagnostic equipment to speed up, lessen, and improve the work of the auto repairman; and credit cards to substitute a single credit decision for the many elaborate, costly, repetitive, labor-intensive, and often dignity-destroying activities and decisions that retail purchases and bank loans formerly entailed. Even that most celebrated and isolated knowledge worker, the scholar, now has at his disposal a computerized research service that provides in minutes a perfect hard-copy citation of every professional journal reference of every single publication by, say, Peter F. Drucker. If Drucker were a chemist, the scholar could also get an abstract of every listed citation. This miracle comes through the courtesy of Lockheed Information Services, a subsidiary of the aeronautics company whose bout with bankruptcy in the mid-1970s was so gleefully cheered by so many condescending scholars. Examples proliferate everywhere, accounting in part for the productivity increases regularly reported in most service activities.

THE NEW SERVICE FECUNDITY

The industrialization of service is still in its infancy. Perhaps the most important aspect of this process, however, is hidden. While computers, credit cards, electric hair dryers, electric hand tools, typewriters, and the like have already produced substantial productivity gains, the involvement of an entirely different facet of industrialization is even more promising: the use of manufacturing rationality, what we now call management, in the service sector. The power tools, jigs, machines, electronic controls, turbines, chemical processors, and all the knowledge that created them do not in themselves explain the productivity of manufacturing. More important is how all these are managed. Only recently has this kind of management systematically entered into the service industry.

For more than a century historians and economists have emphasized inventions and machines to explain economic development, conceptually combining these in the taxonomy of "land, labor, and capital" and later adding the notions of an "acquisitive spirit" and a "congenial state." What has been neglected, except in the disparaged netherworld of business literature, is an account of the rational management of economic processes. Although management has occasionally been treated by respected thinkers such as Max Weber, it has been regarded as a separate sociological topic, under the subheading "bureaucracy." Yet, as we have seen, what makes scientific knowledge, inventions, and machines productive is not their mere existence but how they are used, how they are directed, organized, and managed in a complex manufacturing setting.

Daniel Bell does not, of course, ignore this point, but he does not note its primordial importance. Indeed, he seldom even uses the word "management." (It appears at most peripherally, in casual footnotes quoting trivialities by Lenin and Frederick W. Taylor.) When the word is occasionally used, it is as a passive noun (like "scientist") rather than as a functional discipline (like "science"). The closest Bell comes to a serious recognition of the managerial function is in a solitary one-line reference to "professional administrators"—significant in itself, because if management is anything, it is *not* administration. Management selects ends and means; it organizes, plans, directs, controls, and motivates. Administration merely executes.

When facts and logic push Bell's analysis into the general vicinity of managerial activities, his description substitutes strained circumspection for practical familiarity. Historically, according to Bell, "productivity as a concept became possible only through a new 'supporting system' which dictated the placement of machines in a new way. To put the matter less abstractly, modern industrial society is a product of two 'new men,' the engineer and the economist." Bell writes that the engineer designs and arranges machines in the "one best way," while "the economist introduces a calculus of monetary costs, within a framework of relative prices, as a means of finding the most appropriate mix of men and machines in the organization of production."

It is not disrespectful to suggest that no known economist of any academic stature ever came within even telescopic range of the practical labor of production. The economist came *after,* not before, the industrial system. Yet Bell asserts more than once the putative priority of the economist's view in the history of industrial affairs: "With economics comes a rational division of labor, specialization of functions, complementarity of relations, the use of production functions . . . programming . . . etc." Historically, this puts the cart before the horse. Adam Smith first wrote about such notions in 1776, but they were drawn from his observations of what already existed. It is surely significant that Smith's *Wealth of Nations* begins on the very first page not with theories or prescriptions but with a description of the division of labor in pinmaking, an enterprise already in existence, the result not of the theories of an economist but of the imagination and enterprise of a practical manufacturer who simply did what seemed sensible. Linking economics and economists to the success of the industrial system while completely ignoring the work of organizers and managers describes not history but instead our own tendency to prefer formal conceptual schemes over plain labor.

The involvement of modern management in the service sector has already substantially altered the conclusions suggested by the concept of the "postindustrial" society. The conspicuous absence in the service sector of the manufacturing mode of thought described by Adam Smith—this practical rationality we call management—accounts for much of the historical lag of the service sector behind the industrial sector and, indeed, the lag of some industrial societies behind others. This conspicuous absence in history has been matched only by scholarly neglect of the subject of management. Yet some examples will illustrate how management, which is itself a technology (though a "soft" technology), is being "rediscovered" and employed to raise vastly the productivity of the service sector.

"FAST FOOD" TECHNOLOGY

Take the case of food. Most of us buy most of it in the supermarket, a part of the retailing branch of the service sector. It represents an enormous advance in productivity over the corner grocery store, where a single clerk filled an order one item at a time while the customer waited. The supermarket substitutes fast and efficient self-service for the slow, inefficient, and often erratic clerk. The customer is a cooperating agent in the production process—and this is also the case with laundromats, cafeterias, and, more traditionally, schools and churches, where study and prayer by the "customer" of education and religion help produce the products themselves.

The supermarket is obviously more efficient than its predecessor. Interestingly, it models the automotive assembly line. The final product (in this case, the parcel of purchased goods) is assembled from the product inventory of the store, just as a car is assembled from the parts inventory of the factory. Though the customer does most of the production work, customer satisfaction is higher. The supermarket is a triumph of entrepreneurship and management over immemorial custom. On the other hand, take the case of food that is eaten out. Consider McDonald's, to which I refer briefly in Chapter 3 on "The Industrialization of Service." It merits further emphasis in the present context.

Few of today's successful new commercial ventures have antecedents that are more humble and less glamorous. Yet the thriving nationwide chain of McDonald's hamburger outlets is a supreme example of the application of manufacturing and industrial systems in a service industry. Between 1961 and 1981 McDonald's annual sales exploded from $54 million to $7.1 billion. During this remarkable ascent, the White Castle chain, whose name had been practically synonymous throughout the land with low-priced, quick-service hamburgers, practically vanished.

The explanation of the thundering success of McDonald's is not a purely fiscal one, e.g. the argument that it was heavily financed by independent local entrepreneurs who brought to their operations a quality of commitment and energy not com-

173

monly found among hired workers. Nor is it purely geographic, e.g. the argument that each outlet draws its patronage from a relatively small area, thus enabling the number of outlets to multiply easily and quickly. The relevant explanation must deal with the central question of why each individual McDonald's outlet is so predictably successful, why each is so certain to attract so many repeat customers.

Most important are the customer-satisfying consequences of the carefully controlled execution of each outlet's central function—the rapid delivery of a uniform, high-quality mix of low-priced prepared foods in an environment of cleanliness, order, and cheerful courtesy. The systematic substitution of equipment for people, the carefully planned positioning and use of technology, and the meticulous management and use of labor enable McDonald's to attract and hold patronage to a degree no predecessor or imitator has managed to duplicate.

Consider the remarkable ingenuity of the system, which is worth examining in some detail. To start with the obvious, raw hamburger patties are carefully premeasured and prepackaged in a capital-intensive central commissary, thus leaving neither the franchisee nor his employees any discretion as to size, quality, or consistency. This kind of carefully controlled attention is given to all McDonald's products and activities. Each outlet's storage and preparation space and related facilities are expressly designed for, and limited to, a predetermined mix of products: There is now space for any food, beverage, or service that was not designed into the system at the outset. There is not even a sandwich knife or a decent place to keep it. Thus the operator has no discretion regarding what can be sold—not because of contractual limitations, but because of facilities limitations. And the employees have virtually no discretion regarding how to prepare and serve products. McDonald's restaurants are factories in the field, designed and equipped to do only what the planners intended, nothing more or less.

Discretion is the enemy of order, of standardization, and in this case of quality. An automobile assembly line worker who has discretion and latitude might possibly produce a more personalized car, but it would certainly be less reliable. The elabo-

174

rate care taken in designing the automobile, making its components, and structuring and controlling the assembly line is what produces quality cars at low prices—with extraordinary functional reliability, considering that the average new assembly line produces more than one completely ready-to-drive car every single minute of its operation. McDonald's operates precisely the same way. Like Henry Ford's Model T, McDonald's owes much of its success to the conscious design of an industrial system productive enough to offer abundance and quality at bargain-basement, customer-attracting prices. That was its original goal, and that has been its spectacular achievement. It was no accident.

THE McDONALD'S "MACHINE"

To understand and appreciate the McDonald's revolution in service, consider the handling of that uniquely plebian American delicacy, french-fried potatoes. French fries quickly become soggy and unappetizing; to be crisp and tasty, they must be fresh, made just before eating. McDonald's provides its outlets with precut, partially-cooked frozen potatoes that can be quickly finished in a deep-fry facility on the premises. That is the first step in the process of industrialization, just as Detroit provides the assembly line worker with parts and tools.

The McDonald's fryer is neither so large that it produces too many french fries at one time (thus allowing them to become stale or soggy) nor so small that it requires frequent and costly frying. The fryer is emptied onto a wide, flat tray adjacent to the service counter. This location is crucial. Since the practice of McDonald's is to create an impression of abundance and generosity by slightly over-filling each bag of french fries, the tray's location next to the service counter prevents spillage from reaching the floor. Spillage creates not only danger underfoot but also an unattractive appearance that causes the employees to become accustomed to an unclean environment. Once a store is unclean in one area, standards fall rapidly, and the store becomes unclean and the food unappetizing.

While McDonald's aims for an impression of abundance, excessive overfilling could be very costly for a company that annually buys potatoes almost by the trainload. A systematic bias that puts into each bag even a half ounce more than is intended could have visibly depressing effects on the company's earnings. Further, excessive time spent at the tray by the employees could create a cumulative service bottleneck at the counter.

McDonald's therefore developed a special wide-mouthed scoop with a narrow funnel in its handle. The counter employee picks up the scoop and inserts the handle end into a wall clip containing the bags; a single bag then adheres to the handle. In one continuous movement, the employee fills the scoop with potatoes, and then fills the bag—with the exact amount its designers intended—by lifting the scoop toward the ceiling, so that the potatoes funnel through the handle into the attached bag, which is automatically disengaged by the weight of the contents. The bag then comes to a steady rest, on its flat bottom, on the counter.

Nothing can go wrong: The employee never soils his hands, the floor remains clean, dry, and safe, and the quantity is controlled. Best of all, the customer gets a visibly generous portion with great speed, the employee remains efficient and cheerful, and the general impression is one of extravagantly good service.

Consider other aspects of the technology of McDonald's. The tissue to wrap each hamburger is color-coded to denote the mix of condiments. Heated reservoirs hold prepared hamburgers for rush demand. Frying surfaces have spatter guards to prevent soiling of the cooks' uniforms. Nothing is left to chance or the employees' discretion.

The entire system is engineered and executed according to a tight technological discipline that ensures fast, clean, reliable service in an atmosphere that gives the modestly paid employees a sense of pride and dignity. In spite of the crunch of eager customers, no employee looks or acts harassed, and therefore no harassment is communicated to the customers.

But McDonald's goes even further. Customers may be discouraged from entering if the building looks unappealing from the outside. Hence considerable care goes into the design and appearance of the establishment. Some things, however, the architect cannot control, especially at a restaurant where people eat in their parked cars and are likely to drop hamburger wrappings and empty beverage cartons on the ground. McDonald's has anticipated the problem: Its blacktop parking lots are dotted like a chessboard with numerous large, highly visible trash cans, whose purpose is impossible to ignore. Even the sloppiest customer would be embarrassed to drop his trash on the ground. But just in case someone does, the larger McDonald's outlets have motorized sweepers for quick and easy cleanup. Employees are much more eager to clean the parking lot by riding a motorized sweeper than by using a nail on a stick.

McDonald's has created a highly sophisticated piece of service technology by applying the manufacturing mode of managerial thought to a labor-intensive service situation. If a machine is a piece of equipment with the capability of producing a predictably standardized, customer-satisfying output while minimizing the operating discretion of its attendant, that is what a McDonald's outlet is. It produces, with the help of totally unskilled machine tenders, a fairly sophisticated, reliable product at great speed and low cost.

McDonald's represents the industrialization of service, applying through management the same systematic modes of analysis, design, organization, and control that are commonplace in manufacturing. These more than anything else account for its success. We have already noted the relationship in beauty shops between productivity and demand, and demand and product innovation. The same is true of McDonald's. The control of production and quality through careful systems design creates the demand that justifies the managerial expense, which in turn improves the McDonald's "machine" and expands its commercial domain—to the greater glory of productivity statistics in the food-service sector.

MANAGERIAL RATIONALITY

Precisely the same sort of applied rationality has been used to improve the distribution and service of industrial products. In

1961 the Building Controls and Components Group of Honeywell, Inc., the nation's largest producer of heating and air-conditioning thermostats and control devices, did a major part of its business in replacement controls (the "aftermarket"). These were sold through heating and air-conditioning distributors, who then supplied plumbers and other installation and repair specialists. At that time Honeywell's product line consisted of nearly 18,000 separate catalog parts and pieces. The company had nearly 5,000 distributor accounts, none of which could economically carry a full line of these items. Honeywell therefore maintained nearly a hundred fully stocked field warehouses that offered immediate delivery to distributors. The result was that distributors frequently sold to plumbers parts that they did not themselves have in stock. They either sent plumbers to nearby Honeywell warehouses for pickup or picked up parts themselves and delivered them directly to the plumbers. The costs of carrying these inventories were enormous but were considered a normal expense of doing business.

Then Honeywell made a daring move. It announced its new Tradeline Policy. It would close all warehouses, and all parts would have to be stocked by the distributors. The original equipment, however, had been redesigned in the meantime to use 300 standard, interchangeable parts—interchangeable for most Honeywell controls and also for many of its major competitors. Moreover, each package was clearly imprinted to show exactly which products made by Honeywell or its competitors the contents were compatible with.

By closing its own warehouses, Honeywell obviously shifted the inventory carrying costs to its distributors. But instead of imposing new burdens on them, the new interchangeable products enabled distributors to carry substantially smaller inventories, particularly by cutting down the need for stocking the replacement parts for competitors' products, which the distributors could nonetheless continue to service. Thus they were able to offer their customers faster service at lower costs. Repairs, moreover, could be done more easily and more cheaply.

Honeywell's replacement market share almost doubled, its original equipment share rose by nearly 50 percent, and its trade inventory carrying costs were cut to zero. Whereas previously nearly 90 percent of Honeywell's replacement sales were scattered among 4,000 distributors, within ten years after the introduction of the new policy the same proportion—but of a doubled volume—was concentrated among only about 900 vastly more effective distributors.

What was considered an inescapably labor-intensive problem was solved by the scrupulous application of manufacturing managerial methods. Motivation, hard work, personalization, training, and merchandising incentives were replaced by a revised selection of goals and purposes—not raising sales but creating conditions that would make distributors *want* to expand their dealings with Honeywell at substantially reduced costs to Honeywell itself. The basic management decision to focus with imagination on the service problems and needs of the company's distributors and their customers was the starting point. Service became faster, easier, and cheaper not because of good administration but because of superb management.

Similar thinking is now being used in commercial fields, e.g., as previously noted, by the Transamerica Title Insurance Corporation in its industrialization of the formerly complex, one-to-one, labor-intensive activities needed to deliver low-cost, accurate property title searches and guarantees to its clients.

These examples of the industrialization of service through the application of managerial rationality—McDonald's, credit cards, supermarkets, Transamerica, and others—are neither trivial nor exceptional, selectively plucked out of an otherwise drab reality to suggest speculative possibilities with limited probabilities. They illustrate possibilities that have for the service sector today the same irrepressible potential (even inevitability) that was once characteristic of pinmaking, which Adam Smith used as an example in 1776 to illustrate the division of labor and all that it implied for manufacturing.

PRODUCTION VERSUS PERFORMANCE

The historical absence of industrial modes of managerial thought largely accounts for the sluggishness of so many service industries. There is a reason for that absence, and it is well to understand it.

The word "service" evokes timeworn images of personal ministration and attendance. Its etymological brethren are "servile" and "servitude." "Service" generally refers to deeds performed personally (and humbly) for another. It carries historical connotations of obedience, subordination, and subjugation or of charity, gallantry, and selflessness. In these contexts, people serve because they have to (as in slavery, or such roles of attendance as waiter, maid, bellboy, or cleaning lady).

In the higher-status service occupations, such as in the church and the army, one customarily behaves ritualistically, not rationally. In the lower-status service occupations, one simply obeys. In neither is independent thinking considered a requisite of the job. The most that could therefore be expected in the way of improvements is that, like Avis, service workers would try harder. They would exert more animal effort to do better what they are already doing. They are impotently tethered to ancient, preindustrial modes of thought.

In manufacturing, by contrast, the orientation is toward the efficient production of results, not toward ritual or attendance on others. Relationships are strictly businesslike, with fewer invidious social connotations of rank or class. In the manufacturing cognitive mode, the search for improvement seldom focuses on ways to improve personal performance in present tasks but rather on discovering entirely new ways of performing present tasks or, better yet, on actually changing the tasks themselves. The manufacturing routine is not to think of the greater exertion of animal energies (working physically harder, as the slave), of greater commitment (being more devout or loyal, as the priest), or of greater dependency (being more obsequious, as the butler). Instead, it involves the greater exertion of the mind. In its simplest form, the question is what kinds of tools, old or new, what different materials, or what kinds of skills, processes, organizational rearrangements, incentives, controls, and audits might be enlisted to improve greatly the intended outcome. Often the problem is turned inside out: Does the intended outcome really correspond to the problems its users are trying to solve? Might the problem be redefined or the tool redesigned to make it faster or cheaper, while improving its quality and effectiveness? In short, manufacturing looks for solutions *inside* the very tasks to be done and problems to be solved—not simply the manufacturing task but also the user's problems. That is precisely what Henry Ford did so successfully. He turned the problem inside out, converting a costly constructed machine into an inexpensive assembled one, converting a class market into a mass market.

Contrast the cognitive modes of manufacturing with those of the service industries, where solutions are sought not *inside* the tasks but in their *performance*. Until very recently inherited attitudes and ancient cognitive modes sought impotently for possible improvement in the skills and attitudes of the *performers* of service rather than for possible redefinition or redesign of service itself.

Manufacturing has outperformed service because it has for a long time thought technocratically and managerially about its functions. Service has lagged because it has thought humanistically. Since all of us are human, and none machines, that is an unappetizing pill to swallow. Yet regardless of what we would like, it is inescapable that as long as we think in largely humanistic rather than technocratic terms, the service sector of the modern economy will forever lag. So long as we view service as invariably personal, as something performed entirely by personal effort or by the dedication of individuals for the direct benefit of other individuals, we are prevented from seeking alternatives to the use of people. Such thinking prevents us from redesigning the tasks themselves; from entertaining revised purposes; from creating new plans, tools, processes, systems, organizations, or controls; perhaps even from eliminating the conditions that created the problems in the first place.

PRODUCTIVE PROTOTYPES

To improve the quality and efficiency of service takes the kind of technocratic thinking that in other fields has replaced the high cost and erratic elegance of the artisan with the low cost and predictable munificence of the manufacturer. It requires, in short, the industrialization of service. This is now rapidly happening, though not without frequent setbacks stemming generally from elegant technocrats who promise too much too soon. (Not everybody wants to eat at McDonald's, though it sometimes looks that way. Not everything is equally accessible to industrial rationality, though more is than meets the casual eye.) We have already referred, as additional examples of new industrializing modes, to the Mr. Mini shoe repair shops in Continental Europe, to Damon Corporation's pathological clinics throughout the nation, and to the health maintenance organizations that provide low-cost, prepaid outpatient medical services at clinics manned by almost every conceivable kind of medical specialist—highly paid, salaried employees freed from all the troublesome administrative details of ordinary practice. We have also noted the ambulatory surgical facilities that perform operations on healthy, low-risk patients at remarkably low cost and with enormous speed and ease.

Similarly we have seen similar industrializing economies and speeds achieved by lawyers with access to computerized legal search systems. Enjoying still greater popularity are the new so-called boutique law services that specialize in providing conventional searches and only that; they do not practice law. Significantly, this is the same kind of specialization that explains why General Motors does not make its own tires, windows, or various other parts: It is a "manufacturing" corporation whose manual work consists largely of assembling what it has bought, like Sears, Roebuck when it fills a mail order or the American Express Company with its wide line of packaged travel tours, produced and managed by others, a supermarket of tours fully explained in a regularly published book in clear, technicolor detail. Travelers know what they'll get and the exact cost, and everything is prearranged, including options to permit custom-tailored vacations, not unlike buying a "customized" car by ordering options in the showroom. And how much simpler and cheaper such a travel service is than the alternative: agonized and costly travel arrangements made by yourself or by a travel agent whose reliability is questionable, knowledge limited, and avarice limitless.

THE LIMITS OF INDUSTRIALIZATION

The industrialization of the service-sector industries, and hence the enhancement of their productivity, is just now crawling out of infancy and seems on its way to adolescence. As in human adolescence, there will surely be much abortive experimentation and trauma, but many industries will grow and prosper. Some already have. Knowledge, the most transferrable of all resources, seems finally on the verge of making its greatest contribution to our living standards, not so much by the invention of things for the service sector to use as by the reconsideration of goals and purposes and the application of rational calculation, systems, and routines and by the use of management in their direction and control. The "postindustrial" society already has some productive prototypes, and McDonald's is not the only one.

But some things are less easily managed than others. The demand for many service activities—food service, banking, retailing, amusement places, and the like—often fluctuates widely at particular hours of the day and among days of the week. During nonpeak times there is usually idle capacity. If demand were spaced out, it might substantially raise productivity; however, that cannot be easily managed. Entertainment places and some restaurants try to manage it by differential pricing: reduced prices for Wednesday night movies, reduced midweek prices at ski resorts, ladies' day at ballgames, "happy hour" bargain drinks that start at 3:00 P.M. Moreover, many people are in service because it offers more opportunities for self-employment: professional occupations, retailing, repair. Self-employment is more than twice as common in service as in the rest of the economy. Where self-employment is the main motivation, managerial efficiency takes a back seat, or at least not the driver's seat. The owner is less likely to make capital-intensive or management-intensive improvements than the professional manager with a different set of motivations. Where income is traded for "freedom," productivity will probably lag. Victor Fuchs's studies show that within the same service sectors worker productivity is higher in firms with employees than in firms where the proprietor (and possibly his family) does all the work. In part, the difference is the result of economies of scale —bigger firms are less likely to be proprietor-operated. In part, it reflects the superiority of the professionally managed enterprise. Since there will always be those who would rather earn less than work for others, the superior productivity of competitors will never destroy all those who are less efficient. Small corner grocery stores, small repair shops, and small accounting offices survive, even though their self-employed owners often work for incomes pitifully exploitative on a per-hour basis and generally small also on an absolute basis. This is seldom possible in manufacturing.

Productivity in the intangible goods sector will therefore, on the average, remain lower than tangible goods productivity, even when service becomes more industrialized. But it is not the hopeless structural case it is widely believed to be. Not even in government.

THE SPECIAL CASE
OF GOVERNMENT

Over 18 percent of the American employed work force is now in government, federal, state, and local. Government is the most heavily labor-intensive portion of the intangible-goods sector. It is correct to give it special attention for two reasons: Little of its work is assumed to have access to the productivity-improving technology of the goods-producing industries, and it is assumed to be incorrigibly resistant to reduction in size; indeed, it is assumed to be continually expanding. Neither assumption may, however, be completely justified.

First, nobody knows what the productivity of government really is. The experts cannot even agree how to measure it. The result, unbelievable but true, is the official assumption that the productivity of government work neither rises nor falls; the reported data thus show no productivity changes, year in and year out. Second, if productivity can rise in finance, insurance, and real estate management, as it did between 1929 and 1961 (lagging behind the average increase of the total economy by only 0.26 percent), then it can rise in government, where the nature of the work is often very similar. Third, the notion that government (or, for that matter, any white-collar work) can be managed and rationalized just as can blue-collar work is relatively new. Frederick W. Taylor made his original time-and-motion studies on workers hauling slag and limestone for Midvale Steel Company in Pennsylvania in 1881. What eventually resulted were "scientific management," piecework compensation, and much more that has vastly raised the productivity of manufacturing. Now that white-collar workers (in and out of government) have conceded their proletarian status by joining labor unions, they have opened the gates to similar managerial intrusions in their work. It was not until 1975 that a manual was written on how to use Taylor's ninety-four-year-old methods to enhance productivity in government and service organizations —and then it was the Japanese who published it.[2] It was not until the adoption of the "Federal Reorganization Plan No. 2" of 1970 that the federal government was required to pay some official attention to developing the managerial skills of its civil service executives. Now each manager in civil service "super-grades" 16 to 28 must receive at least one week of formal management training. Middle managers in grades 13 to 15 are now required to receive two weeks. That is a beginning; unfortunately, it involves only the federal government. Of the nation's 16 million nonmilitary governmental employees in 1981, 13.2 million were in local and state governments.

The spectacle of an ever increasing number of government employees is, in fact, duplicated in the entire service sector. Between 1950 and 1974 the number of employed service workers rose 90 percent, and that of goods-producing workers only 34

[2] Marvin E. Mundel, *Measuring and Enhancing the Productivity of Service and Government Organizations* (Tokyo: Asian Productivity Organization, 1975).

percent. Between 1970 and 1981 the number in goods-producing industries rose 10 percent, and in non-goods-producing industries 39 percent. Indeed, as a proportion of the total labor force, service employment has been rising without interruption since 1880 (though not uniformly: The proportion for the railroads started falling in 1947; the proportion for real estate in 1974 was even with that of 1956). The difference is that the proportion for government has risen faster than any other, up from 13 percent of the employed labor force in 1950 to 18 percent now. This increase has come largely from three sources: from the rising role of government in national affairs that started with the Great Depression; from the increase in the permanent military establishment (both in uniform and out) that resulted from the beginning of the Cold War in 1948 and the subsequent buildup for the Korean War in 1951; but mostly from the "New Frontier" and "Great Society" programs that started in 1961 at the federal level and then quickly spread through all levels of government.

There is a special argument about government. It is widely believed that government employment is uniquely resistant to reduction for several reasons: (1) the public wants increasingly more public services; (2) the "military–industrial complex" and generalized xenophobia will keep armaments spending up; (3) the government is run by its permanent cadre who ensure their own permanence; and (4) civil service employment and seniority rules are equivalent to employment guarantees; that is, even if labor-saving technologies and systems were available, the high-seniority officials (those with the most power) will be the last to go and the last to change, for age and inertia are on their side. If white-collar work is ever sufficiently rationalized to raise efficiency and cut employment, government will take at least a generation longer to do likewise. Government will always necessarily lag.

The third and fourth reasons are essentially the same and probably about as true in government as elsewhere. Even private industry has a seniority system, institutionalized in the lower-level and middle-level white-collar ranks, rationalized in the upper ranks, and veiled behind a windy rhetoric tough-mindedly claiming the opposite. More things often happen where they are not supposed to happen than where they are.

The second reason, the persistence of high military spending, is contradicted by all of history. In fact, military spending, despite its absolute magnitude, declines proportionately, and always has in the long run. United States defense outlays fell from 8.4 percent of GNP in 1946 (at its peak in 1968 during the Vietnam War it was 9.4 percent) to 5.9 percent in 1974. In 1982 outlays were, in constant dollars, below the levels of the early 1960s.

THE "DEMOCRATIC DISTEMPER"

As for the first reason, the analysis of Samuel P. Huntington is especially useful.[3] He refers to the "democratic distemper" of the 1960s: the simultaneous increase in the demand for and the actual amount of government activity on the one hand, and the decline of government authority on the other. During what Huntington calls the "democratic surge" of the 1960s, one opinion poll after another showed that public confidence in the leadership of the President, the Congress, the Supreme Court, and the military declined almost in proportion to the expansion of their activities. Though the public wanted more government and was passionately involved in getting more, the more it got, the less it liked what it got. While the authority of government has been restored somewhat in the 1980s, it still lacks the authority it had in the 1950s. The general faith in the capacity of government to achieve many of the democratic, liberal, and egalitarian goals generated by the "democratic surge" of the 1960s is in tatters. Expanding upon Huntington, we can say that the disillusionment probably began about 1969, principally among the liberal intellectuals in the universities. In their introductory essay to *The Public Interest* special issue (Winter 1974) on the "Great Society," Eli Ginzberg and Robert M. Solow, both sensitive and ardent advocates of a more benign society and supporters of a more meliorative state, wrote regarding the programs of the 1960s that "the attack that was finally launched

[3] Samuel P. Huntington, *American Politics: The Promise of Disharmony* (Cambridge: Harvard University Press, 1981). See also his article, "The Democratic Distemper," *The Public Interest,* No. 41 (Fall 1975), pp. 9–38.

by the conservatives was if anything overdue. . . . But more surprising was the growing disillusionment and despair of many of the social architects of these intervention programs and of the constituencies for which they spoke."

Intellectuals understandably believe that what they write has some effect, sooner or later. In the past, egalitarianism and the expansion of government services have defined their advocacy. In time the public followed. Now the public again follows —this time, leadership in the opposite direction. No matter, however, who leads and who follows, the direction seems clear. Historic precedent is, furthermore, on the side of a reversal of attitudes. Huntington notes:

> During periods of rapid social change . . . democratic and egalitarian values of the American creed are reaffirmed. The intensity of belief during such "creedal passion periods" leads to the challenging of established authority and to major efforts to change governmental structure to accord more fully with those values. In this respect . . . the democratic surge of the 1960s shares many characteristics with the comparable egalitarian and reform movements of the Jacksonian and Progressive eras. Those "surges," like the contemporary one, also occurred during periods of realignment between party and governmental institutions on the one hand, and social forces on the other. The slogans, goals, values, and targets of all these movements are strikingly similar. Consequently, the implication of this analysis is that in due course the democratic surge and the resulting dual distemper in government will be moderated.

There is already a clear reduction in political activity (though not so much in political noise) in the nation, and it is not simply that an unpopular war is over and an ineffectual President is out. Most people increasingly seem to feel that things haven't worked and that the costs have gone out of sight. Finally, the plight of major cities has made things so bad that everybody not just accepts but insists upon limits and reductions. Michael Dukakis, an attractive and intelligent liberal Democrat, was elected Governor of Massachusetts in 1974 on a traditionally liberal ticket. Even then within three weeks of taking office he got tough-minded, saying in essence, "We can't afford it. Things haven't worked. We will cut back, and the budget will be balanced." In eight months he had cut 8,000 from the welfare rolls, reduced state employment, and just about balanced the budget.

Anyone who reads the political commentaries and public sentiments in the local newspapers and hears what is said on the public streets, in the offices and factories, and at local government meetings cannot escape the accumulating evidence of a repudiation of governmental efficacy. People simply want less government and want it to try nothing new, except, perhaps, for fiscal and monetary policies to prop up the economy and programs for the aged, infirm, and the clearly dispossessed. Those are central to their lives; all the rest is suspect, unless people are direct beneficiaries of a particular largesse. And even then the sentiment for "getting mine" is weakening. Indeed, it is not clear that there ever was wide support for all the "Great Society" programs that went into such rapid shambles and disrepute.

The meaning seems clear enough. The percentage of the total employed labor force in government was declining even before President Reagan, as it declined in the Eisenhower years, not only because the labor force is now expanding but because government employment has been shrinking absolutely. This will certainly moderate whatever structural tendency exists toward declining rates of productivity, slower economic growth, and rising inflation.

POSSIBILITIES FOR PROGRESS

Most government services certainly are different, functionally and qualitatively, from most private sector services. The technology of management—or management as a form of knowledge—is less easily accessible to some service activities than to others. To that extent, the attempt to expand productivity in the service sector will be more difficult and less rewarding in many cases than in most of the goods-producing sector. The work of the surgeon may be facilitated by better equipment and

189

organization in the operating room, but he can hardly do two appendectomies in the time it has always taken him to do one. The government interviewer at the unemployment compensation office is not likely to have access to the productivity-improving technologies that created the applicant before him.

On the other hand, there may be more possibilities than meet the casual eye. It is noteworthy, for example, that a large proportion of the continually increasing number of applications for credit cards and small loans are "processed" not by time-consuming personal interviews or application reviews but by simple, fast (not even computerized), one-page credit-scoring forms. The score coefficients that measure credit-worthiness on these applications are developed through statistically sophisticated sensitivity analysis; the "cutoff" and "acceptance" points are determined with the help of Bayesian statistics. Significantly, this rapid scoring system was the development not of banks, finance companies, department stores, petroleum companies, or the American Express Company, but of rank outsiders, trained in systems analysis, who recognized and capitalized on an opportunity to make a dollar—knowledge workers who created a service company to enhance the productivity of other service companies.

Though such a development has made "interviewing" for credit purposes more productive than interviewing for unemployment compensation purposes, it's unlikely this sort of mechanization, no matter how efficient, will be readily tolerated at the unemployment office. Just as there are differences between types of service industries, so there are differences in their susceptibility to industrialization. Technical possibility is not equivalent to practical acceptability.

But to say this is to concede nothing. We saw that the goods-producing industries have not been homogeneously productive, ranging on an annual growth basis between 1948 and 1966 from 1.1 percent for the manufacturing of tobacco products to 4.9 percent for chemicals. So also in service: between 1939 and 1963 from 0.6 percent annually for barber shops to 3.3 percent annually for auto repairs.

The theory of the "postindustrial" society conjures frightening apprehensions about the future, a structural transformation leading to reduced productivity and heightened inflation. Substantively, however, this has almost nothing to do with the rise of the knowledge worker, as is claimed. When goods-producing industries outproduced the service industries in the nineteenth century and the first half of the twentieth, the absence of theoretical or science-based knowledge did not keep the "tinkerers" from making their Brobdingnagian progress. Only by assuming that theoretical knowledge will necessarily be more productive in the future than practical knowledge ("tinkering") has been in the past is there any basis for asserting that the difference in the kind of knowledge *per se* will produce a vast new difference in productivity between the goods and service industries.

Nothing in actual experience would comfortably lead one to this conclusion. It has now been more than twenty-five years since fusion physics was proved theoretically feasible and more than ten years since it was proved practically feasible in the laboratory. But widespread safe use is decades distant—all it takes in the meantime to make it work is practical technologists, "tinkerers," if you will.

Similarly, Dennis Gabor received the Nobel Prize for his development of holography just after World War II. In the early 1960s the RCA Corporation, with all the vast resources at its command, made a concerted effort to produce a commercially acceptable holographic film and motion picture–making process. The prize was huge: all of Eastman Kodak, all of the Hollywood and television tape market, the entire still and motion picture camera market, and an entirely new market calculated in the billions—low-priced home television tape players and tape cassettes. Ten years and several hundred million dollars later, the effort, for all practical purposes, was scrapped. It began with theoretical knowledge, but it foundered on the failure of economically justifiable practicality, "tinkering," if you will. The engineers and technicians, blessed with assorted university degrees and masterships in toolmaking, and working day and night under ideal conditions, with superb facilities, at Princeton, New Jersey, failed, just as John F. Kettering, also a master

191

toolmaker, failed so miserably in the 1920s to create his dream of an entirely revolutionary alternative to the carburetor. Two generations later, scientists at General Motors had meanwhile taken Kettering's place, with no results. The most they have been able to do is to use a microprocessor to monitor and improve the mechanical mixing of fuel and air in the same old carburetor or improve on direct fuel injection.

The knowledge required to create holography is based on science and theory, constructed step by step from the accumulation of other science and theory. And although modern science-based industries may begin with scientific theory, if they are characterized in practice by any one thing, it is precisely that their results were *not* attained through, nor do they end with, theory. The "tinkerers" are more necessary now than ever. The "cookers" in microcircuit production are the rule, not the exception, in science-based industries.

THE PRACTICE OF MANAGEMENT

The rise of science-based industries and the importance of the knowledge worker have no structurally unique significance or effects. What is significant is that in the more advanced societies abundance and affluence create proportionately increased demands for things less easily produced under the conditions of mass-production efficiency. But the recent increased demand for handcrafted artifacts—from "folk" jewelry to "antique" executive desks—tells us that even in the goods-producing industries mass-production efficiency does not exhaust all the public's oscillating wants.

Increasingly more of what is wanted, however, is services. As in the case of beauty shops, credit cards, hamburgers, after-market repairs of thermostats, medicine, or law, it is reasonable to assume that when markets expand the managerial imagination will apply its own kind of special knowledge to raise productivity.

Whatever else may have changed, the "postindustrial" society is not "post" in the sense that expanding bursts of industrialization are past. Industrialization is more than inventions, machines, and amassed technology. Among the growing proportion of "knowledge workers" are not just engineers, scientists, and technicians but, more importantly, managers. The fleeting references to managers in the literature of the "postindustrial" society are but grudging concessions. What is assumed to be decisive is the expanding scientific elite, with its "systematic development of research and the creation of (disproportionately productive) science-based industries" that are presumed to help produce profound structural imbalances in our society. This lyrical account of science overlooks the fact that science-based industries were "created," "developed," and made "systematic" by somebody, that the "joining of science to invention, principally through the organization of research and development efforts" still depends, heavily and inescapably, on the practical labors of honest "tinkerers" and above all on the work of managers who identify problems and opportunities, define goals and purposes, select means, marshal resources, motivate, energize, direct, measure, control, and reward the performance of people.

All that management did in the past to make technology and abundance possible in the goods-producing industries, and all it is now doing to help convert scientific knowledge into the practical output of technological systems—all this is now in ascendance in the non-goods-producing industries. Something of what can be achieved has already been described. More is surely on the way.

Management is a crucial element of society. If society is indeed going to be "postindustrial," the only recent emergence of the managerial arts in the expanding sectors of society suggests the likelihood that these sectors will enjoy the same productivity-improving results in the years ahead that the industrial sectors did in years past. The predicted apocalypse of structural imbalances that will "immiserize" progress is a misperception of the future. It neglects or fails to account for precisely what, in the end, makes economic progress possible: the practice of management.

Index